THE HOGAN GUIDE

THE HOGAN GUIDE

Interpretation and Use of the Hogan Inventories

2nd Edition

Robert Hogan and Joyce Hogan

Printed in the United States of America.

For information, contact Hogan Press
11 S. Greenwood, Tulsa OK 74120
hoganassessments.com

ISBN: 979-8-9856452-8-6

H
HOGANPRESS

Contents

CHAPTER 1
Personality and Assessment 1

CHAPTER 2
The Hogan Personality Inventory 7

CHAPTER 3
How to Interpret the Hogan Personality Inventory 13

CHAPTER 4
Hogan Development Survey 35

CHAPTER 5
How to Interpret the Hogan Development Survey 45

CHAPTER 6
Motives, Values, Preferences Inventory 71

CHAPTER 7
How to Interpret the Motives, Values, Preferences Inventory 79

CHAPTER 8
Configural Interpretation 101

CHAPTER 9
Conflict Interpretation 115

CHAPTER 10
Feedback: The Hogan Way 125

CHAPTER 11
Coaching the Hogan Way 141

Bibliography 157
Index 161

Chapter 1
Personality and Assessment

Overview

The keys to success in business are money and people. People study finance to understand money, and they study personality psychology to understand people. Personality psychology concerns the nature of human nature. Proper talent management depends on two things: (1) some understanding of human nature and (2) the ability to assess its key components. This brings us to Hogan Assessments. This chapter provides a quick introduction to personality assessment, in general, and our assessments, in particular.

Personality

The Hogan inventories (the Hogan Personality Inventory, HPI; the Hogan Development Survey, HDS; and the Motives, Values, Preferences Inventory, MVPI) are unique in that they are based on socioanalytic theory, meaning that they rest on a solid conceptual foundation.

Socioanalytic theory argues that life is about competing for the resources needed to survive while trying to build and support a family. People do this in two ways: (1) They form relationships with others who may share resources with them when necessary, and (2) they compete with others directly for status and resources. This is called *getting along* and *getting ahead*, respectively. Getting along and getting ahead are often incompatible. When people try to get along with others, they usually give up getting ahead, and if they are successful at getting ahead, others tend to resent them, meaning that they are not getting along. Cooperation (getting along) and competition (getting ahead) are frequently incompatible activities, and balancing them requires versatility—a personality characteristic.

People's lives and careers consist of a long series of interactions with other people. After every interaction, people gain or lose some acceptance and/or status. The amount of social respect and status that people enjoy is the result of all their interactions and is reflected in their reputations.

The three Hogan inventories are concerned with how people interact with others and how they pursue their career goals. In very general terms, the HPI concerns the *bright side* of personality—how people are seen by others when they are monitoring their behavior. The HDS concerns the *dark side* of personality—how people are seen by others when they let down their guard and stop monitoring their behavior. The MVPI focuses on core values—what people desire or want to avoid, often in unconscious ways. Finally, the three inventories predict behaviors that contribute to or detract from getting along and getting ahead. Individual differences in a person's ability to get along and get ahead contribute directly to their career success.

The Hogan inventories are unique in that the Hogan Assessments take test validity more seriously than any of its commercial competitors. Taking validity seriously involves providing empirical evidence that an inventory predicts real-world performance. Gathering and providing validity evidence is expensive and time-consuming. While many businesses and organizations may not seem to care about validity, Hogan conducts validity research because it is the right thing to do. Many commercial test publishers sell the psychometric equivalent of snake oil, so as always, *caveat emptor*.

Finally, Hogan stands out because most commercial publishers of personality measures claim that their assessments *measure traits*; in contrast, the Hogan inventories are designed to *predict performance*. We believe that talking about measuring traits is nonsense; predicting performance is essential.

Personality and Job Performance

Why should businesses take personality assessment seriously? Because there are clear financial consequences associated with good versus bad hiring and promotion decisions. Personality assessment is an indispensable tool for rational talent management.

Extensive research indicates that well-validated personality inventories predict every aspect of career performance better than unstructured employment interviews, assessment center exercises, IQ tests, background checks, or polygraph interviews (cf. Dilchert et al., 2007; Heimann et al., 2021; J. Hogan & Holland, 2003; LePine & Van Dyne, 2001; McDaniel et al., 1994; O'Boyle et al., 2012; Roberts et al., 2007; Arthur et al., 2003). Not only does valid personality assessment predict performance better than any other known decision-making method, but personality assessment also does not discriminate against protected classes of job applicants (Hough, 2001): minority applicants score the same as white males; women score the same as men.

People often have strong beliefs that are not true, such as thinking they have a good sense of humor or good taste in food, music, and clothes when this may not be the case. Similarly, many people may think they are good judges of character. However, 50 years of research shows that, on average, most people are poor judges of character. Empirical tests on predicting other people's performance show that validated personality assessments outperform individual judgment in unstructured interviews (Highhouse, 2008). Consequently, when making decisions about people, personality assessment is essential.

Employability refers to the ability to gain and maintain employment or find a new job. Data show that there are strong individual differences in employability that are related to personality (Boudreaux et al., 2022). People are typically hired based on their technical qualifications and fired based on their inability to get along with coworkers. Three broad aspects of personality explain this: (1) Some people are charming and agreeable;

others are moody, irritable, and difficult to live with. (2) Some people are conscientious, dependable, and compliant; others are careless, undependable, and even sneaky and deceitful. (3) Some people are hardworking and take pride in their jobs; others wait to be told what to do. A valid personality assessment easily captures these tendencies.

No matter how charming, talented, or hardworking a person may be, if they do not fit with the job's psychological demands or the organization's values, they will not succeed—for example, a shy introvert working in sales; blunt, impatient person working in customer service; or an extravert working in accounting and information technology. Similarly, a free-thinking artist may struggle to fit into an organization with a militaristic culture, someone concerned with helping less unfortunate may not succeed in investment banking, and a person who dislikes technology will likely flounder at an engineering firm. Personality assessment is the single best way to align individual characteristics with the demands of specific jobs and organizations.

Our research also indicates that 65%–75% of existing managers are likely to fail in one way or another (J. Hogan et al., 2011). This high failure rate occurs for two reasons: On the one hand, organizations typically promote a group's best performer to manager without thinking about whether that person has talent for management; as a result, they lose a good performer and acquire a mediocre manager. On the other hand, organizations often promote managers performing well at one level to a higher level without considering whether they will be able to perform at the next level. Personality assessment is ideally suited for identifying people capable of managing at every level.

Most people would like to improve their performance at work, but the performance feedback they receive is often minimal or unhelpful. Every organizational intervention—including training and development interventions—should be based on a proper assessment. A well-validated personality assessment is an essential guide to performance improvement, but it only works if people truly want to improve.

As this discussion suggests, personality significantly affects people's performance in jobs and organizations, and personality assessment is a key resource for talent management. It allows organizations to assign the right people to the right roles; in turn, that will increase productivity, employee satisfaction, and customer service ratings while minimizing absenteeism, turnover, and other unnecessary personnel costs. In addition, personality assessment is a crucial complement to training and development efforts.

The remainder of this guide covers the three Hogan assessment tools. The discussion is intended to provide insights into how the tools can help solve the practical problems associated with enhancing individual performance, thereby impacting team and broader organizational performance.

Our goal is to provide a useful and helpful guide for interpreting the results of the Hogan inventories, beginning with a brief presentation of how to interpret each of our major inventories:

- Hogan Personality Inventory—a state-of-the-art measure of normal personality designed to reveal the strengths on which a person can build

- Hogan Development Survey—an inventory that captures career derailers—behaviors that impede work relationships, hinder productivity, or limit overall career potential

- Motives, Values, Preferences Inventory—a measure that reveals a person's core values, which are key to work and life satisfaction

Chapter 2
The Hogan Personality Inventory

The Hogan Personality Inventory (HPI) is designed to be used for personnel selection, individualized assessment, and career-related decision-making. It provides detailed information regarding the bright side of personality—tendencies that promote people's ability to get along with others and find occupational success.

Background

Academic personality psychology has adopted the so-called Five Factor Model (FFM) as the definitive taxonomy of personality variables. The FFM is based on more than 90 years of research on the structure of peer ratings (cf. Thurstone, 1934; Tupes & Christal, 1961), and it has been found in most world languages. The FFM suggests that we think about and describe other people in terms of five broad themes (see Table 1) and provides a systematic way to classify individual differences in social behavior. Moreover, overwhelming evidence suggests that all existing personality questionnaires can be described in terms of these five dimensions (e.g., John, 2021). Consequently, the FFM is a crucial starting point for research in personality assessment.

Table 1: The Five-Factor Model

Factor	Description
I. Extraversion	The degree to which a person seems outgoing and assertive
II. Neuroticism	The degree to which a person seems anxious, moody, and easily upset
III. Agreeableness	The degree to which a person seems pleasant and accommodating
IV. Conscientiousness	The degree to which a person seems compliant and conforming
V. Openness to Experience	The degree to which a person seems curious and open-minded

Despite its importance, the FFM has some limitations. For example, the FFM does not adequately account for some significant personality dimensions (i.e., ambition, humility) (e.g., Jones et al., 2017). In addition, the FFM concerns how we think about other people; although people *can* describe themselves in terms of the FFM, they do not normally think of themselves in these terms (Hogan & Blickle, 2013). Rather, people typically think about themselves in terms of their values, goals, aspirations, and fears.

The HPI combines the structure of the FFM with the measurement goals of the California Psychological Inventory (CPI; Gough, 1975), which was for many years the gold standard inventory of normal personality. The CPI was designed to predict important social outcomes, not measure traits. The HPI is what the CPI would be if it were configured in terms of the FFM.

Thus, the FFM tells us about the structure of personality, and the CPI tells us about the goals of assessment—*assessment concerns predicting important social outcomes, not measuring traits*. The HPI was developed to predict job performance.

Initial Development of the HPI

The two big questions in personality assessment are (1) what to measure and (2) how to measure it. The FFM answers the first question: what to measure. Regarding the second question, Hase and Goldberg (1967) demonstrated that, when evaluated in terms of validity, all scale construction methods are similar. This tells us what to measure and how to measure it.

Our viewpoint, socioanalytic theory, also provides a guide to item writing. For each dimension of the FFM, we asked how people might act so as to cause others to rate them as high or low on that dimension. Consider the dimension of Openness to Experience. People with high scores on Openness to Experience seem to be imaginative and curious. This indicates that an Openness to Experience scale should contain items about having unusual ideas and enjoying foreign travel and trendy cuisine. This idea guided us when we wrote items for the HPI, which led to three discoveries.

First, the FFM dimension of Extraversion contains two distinct components: Sociability, concerning whether a person seems to be sociable and outgoing, and Ambition, concerning whether one seems to be driven, competitive, and persistent. Second, the FFM Openness to Experience dimension combines two distinct components: one concerns being curious and imaginative and the other concerns wanting to learn new things. By comparison, each HPI scale is broken down into smaller subthemes. For example, the Adjustment scale contains themes about anxiety, guilt, moodiness, and irritability. We called these subthemes Homogenous Item Composites, or HICs.

We pilot tested the HPI using samples of undergraduate participants and retained items that correlated highly with the other items on each HIC. We continued this process until we had 45 HICs containing 420 items distributed across 7 scales.

Between 1979 and 1984, we assessed more than 1,700 people, including students, hospital workers, U.S. Navy enlisted personnel, clerical workers, truck drivers, sales representatives, police officers, hourly and professional office workers, school administrators, and incarcerated felons. The ages in these samples ranged from 18 to 60. There were 470 women and 1,159 men, 726 Whites and 232 Blacks. Some demographic data were missing. About 20% of the participants were college educated.

Later Development

Using these data, in 1984, we refined each HIC and shortened the inventory to 225 items on 43 HICs; we also retained 85 unscored items for research purposes. Between 1984 and

1992, we tested more than 11,000 people, primarily employed adults in organizations around the United States. Participants' ages ranged from 18 to 67 years, and the sample included 7,061 men and 3,465 women, with a racial/ethnic breakdown of 5,610 White, 1,036 Black, 348 Hispanic, 231 Asian, and 253 Native American participants. Some demographic data were missing. About 20% of the participants in this sample were college-educated. We conducted more than 50 validity studies in various organizations and gathered matched sets of data with other tests, inventories, and observer descriptions.

In 1992, using all our archival data, we conducted a long series of analyses to update the HPI. The 1992 HPI (revised edition) contained seven primary scales and a validity scale. These scales contained a total of 206 items arranged in 41 HICs. No items overlapped on HICs, and no HICs overlapped on scales.

Kaizen Psychometrics

Since the 1990s, we have conducted hundreds of studies using the HPI across a wide range of organizations. We practice what we call Kaizen Psychometrics, a process of continuous improvement based on research-based evidence. This practice is expensive and complicated by translation issues but is also consistent with best practices in all areas of technology.

Since 2002, we have refined the HPI in two ways. First, we have periodically fine-tuned the scoring so that the norms remain reasonably constant over time. In addition, we periodically revised items to ensure that score distributions on all scales continue to approximate normal distributions. We also constantly evaluate samples to ensure scores have no unexpected subgroup differences. We are the only commercial test publisher to practice Kaizen Psychometrics.

In 2023, we moved the HPI and the HDS to a 4-point response format (*Strongly Disagree, Disagree, Agree, Strongly Agree*). The new response format improved the distributions on the HPI scales, their reliability, and their validity, as well as the interpretability of the HICs.

We interpret scores on our scales using normed (percentile) scores because we find that people intuitively understand what a percentile score means. Throughout the years, we have developed large, representative norms for our assessments: the 1995 norms, the General norm (2005), and the Global norm (2011, 2019, 2023). Each norm update used stratification to match the underlying working population on important characteristics such as job category, gender, and assessment purpose (i.e., selection, development). The 2023 Global norm consisted of 159,440 people from 190 countries and territories. As of 2025, we supported local norms in 54 languages.

General Interpretation Guidelines for the HPI

- We typically interpret the HPI in the context of a person's job. Scores that predict success in one job may be less predictive or worse for another job. More importantly, there is no such thing as a good personality profile; profiles should be evaluated in the context of a person's career goals.

- Because interpreting the HPI is job specific, high scores are not necessarily good, and low scores are not necessarily bad. For every dimension, there is good news and bad news associated with high and low scores. Depending on the job, high or low scores may have positive or negative consequences.

- Scores below the 35th percentile are considered low; scores between the 36th and 64th percentile are average, and scores above the 65th percentile are high scores.

- Scales and/or HICs should not be interpreted in isolation; they should always be interpreted in the context of a person's overall profile.

HPI Global Portability

When developing the HPI, we decided early on that we wanted to create the global standard for assessing normal personality. We have pursued this objective for more than 50 years, with the HPI being available in more than 50 languages, including Chinese, Japanese, Indonesian, and Arabic. Research consistently demonstrates that the HPI predicts performance across cultures, languages, and national boundaries (e.g., Hogan & Holland, 2003; Mabon, 1998). Most of the norm differences found in cross-cultural comparisons result from translation or sampling issues.

In conjunction with our international partners, we have expanded our norm data and validation research throughout the global marketplace. We want to offer our customers the industry's best available global research archive so that regardless of cultural boundaries, they can use the HPI with confidence.

At the time of this printing, the HPI is available online in the following languages:

- Arabic
- Azerbaijani
- Bulgarian
- Chinese (Simplified)
- Chinese (Traditional)
- Croatian
- Czech
- Danish
- Dutch
- English (Australian and New Zealand)

- English (Greek)
- English (Indian)
- English (Kenyan)
- English (Middle Eastern)
- English (South African)
- English (UK)
- English (US)
- Estonian
- Finnish
- French (Canadian)
- French (Parisian)
- German
- Greek
- Hebrew
- Hungarian
- Icelandic
- Indonesian
- Italian
- Japanese
- Kazakh
- Korean

- Latvian
- Lithuanian
- Macedonian
- Malaysian
- Montenegrin
- Norwegian
- Polish
- Portuguese (Brazilian)
- Portuguese (European)
- Romanian
- Russian
- Serbian
- Slovak
- Slovenian
- Spanish (Castilian)
- Spanish (Latin American)
- Swedish
- Thai
- Turkish
- Ukrainian
- Vietnamese

Chapter 3

How to Interpret the Hogan Personality Inventory

Scale 1—Adjustment

Adjustment concerns the degree to which a person seems calm and self-accepting or, conversely, moody and self-critical. Key indicators include being cheerful, easygoing, trusting, and forgiving.

Performance Implications of High Scores (65%–100%)

Positive Implications

People with high scores on the Adjustment scale adapt to fast-paced environments and heavy workloads, stay calm under pressure, and rarely overreact or show stress. They seem even-tempered, confident, and poised under pressure. These people rarely worry about past mistakes, trust others, and always look for the positive side of things.

Negative Implications

People with high scores on the Adjustment scale may not realize when others are feeling stressed; as managers, they may pile work on others, not appreciating how this impacts them. They expect to receive only positive feedback and may be hard to coach. These people often seem to lack a sense of urgency and feel they have nothing to prove to anyone. They tend to ignore their mistakes and overestimate their contributions.

Performance Implications of Average Scores (36%–64%)

Positive Implications

People with average scores on the Adjustment scale maintain a good balance between composure and responsiveness. They can remain calm and confident under moderate pressure. They listen to criticism without taking it personally. These people learn from their mistakes and are patient with their staff.

Negative Implications

People with average scores on Adjustment sometimes struggle to find the right balance under stress or uncertainty. High stakes or continuous pressures may cause them to fluctuate between confidence and apprehension. Conversely, they may appear nonchalant and too relaxed about important deadlines.

Tips to consider:

- Those who score on the higher end of average scores tend to remain quite resilient to stress. They accept feedback from others but may be slow to apply it. They may take a more measured approach to work and could be perceived as lacking a sense of urgency.

- Those who score on the lower end of average scores are concerned about their performance and may need more support and reassurance when under stress. They have a reactive work style and may feel a need to prove their worth.

Performance Implications of Low Scores (0%–35%)

Positive Implications

People with low scores on the Adjustment scale are sensitive about how their work will be evaluated and are highly motivated to improve. They often work in bursts of energy and seem to have a sense of urgency. These people usually foresee and proactively address risks or obstacles. They may solicit regular feedback and respond well to coaching.

Negative Implications

People with low scores on the Adjustment scale are tense, moody, and argumentative and may take criticism personally. They might react to stress with noticeable unease. Easily overwhelmed or discouraged by deadlines and heavy workloads, these people might require additional reassurance or emotional support.

Table 2 contains the behavioral implications of low and high scores for the Adjustment scale. Table 3 contains definitions for Adjustment's subscales (i.e., HICs) as well as interpretations for low and high scores. If the assessed individual has a low or average Adjustment score, the subscale scores become more important. Use them to help you interpret the Adjustment score.

Table 2: Behavioral Implications of Adjustment Scores

Low Adjustment Score		High Adjustment Score	
Positive Behaviors	Negative Behaviors	Positive Behaviors	Negative Behaviors
• Emotionally expressive • Candid and honest • Self-aware • Open to feedback • Shows a sense of urgency	• Tense and self-critical • Moody and temperamental • Worrisome and prone to stress • Easily irritated with others • Defensive about work • Takes criticism personally	• Calm and consistent • Handles stress/ pressure well • Self-confident • Even-tempered and upbeat • Patient with others • Won't take criticism personally • Adapts well to changes	• Unable to be self-critical • Ignores negative feedback • Will not take advice • Seems indifferent to deadlines • Can be arrogant • Won't understand when others are stressed

Table 3: Adjustment Subscales Interpretation

Adjustment	Definition	Low Score	High Score
Empathy	Absence of irritability	Irritated by others' faults	Empathic
Not Anxious	Absence of worry	Anxious or tense	Relaxed
No Guilt	Absence of regret	Prone to worrying about past mistakes	No excessive worry about past mistakes
Calmness	Lack of emotionality	Emotional at times	Calm
Even-Tempered	Not moody or irritable	Temperamental or moody	Even-tempered
No Complaints	Positive attitude toward performance	Frequent complaints	Infrequent complaints
Trusting	Not paranoid or suspicious	Questions others' intentions	Trusting
Good Attachment	Good relations with authority	Hostile to authority	Positive attitude toward authority

Scale 2—Ambition

Ambition concerns the degree to which a person seems competitive, persistent, energetic, leaderlike, and upwardly mobile. Key indicators include being confident, bold, assertive, ambitious, and energetic.

Performance Implications of High Scores (65%–100%)

Positive Implications

People with high scores on the Ambition scale are very active, driven, and highly motivated and naturally aspire to leadership positions. Results-oriented, competitive, and persistent, these people are not afraid to fail; they want to achieve impressive results and lead others to challenging goals.

Negative Implications

People with high scores on the Ambition scale can be very concerned about winning, and they may compete against their team and/or direct reports. They are impatient or become frustrated when goals are not quickly met. They are often perceived as too dominant and arrogant, get involved in company politics, and can become restless if they do not get promoted.

Performance Implications of Average Scores (36%–64%)

Positive Implications

People with average scores on the Ambition scale balance personal drive with cooperation. They take the initiative when required but do not feel compelled to lead. They tend to set realistic goals, accept challenges consistent with their skill levels, and are likely seen as reliable team members who support team success.

Negative Implications

People with average scores on the Ambition scale may be reluctant to assert themselves and could miss leadership or advancement opportunities, even if they are desired. These people may struggle to identify when they should take the initiative and lead versus when they should assume a support role and follow.

Tips to consider:

- Those who score on the higher end of average scores are more likely to accept challenging assignments. They may enjoy positions of authority or being responsible for decision-making. However, they could become overly assertive or dominant and ignore input from others.

- Those who score on the lower end of average scores tend to be seen as good team players who are more comfortable taking direction than giving it. They seem to be deferential, compliant, and patient. As managers, they may be reluctant to make decisions on their own and may lack a clear agenda or direction.

Performance Implications of Low Scores (0%–35%)

Positive Implications

People with low scores on the Ambition scale feel more content following others than leading. They do not play company politics and are excellent team players. They are typically patient, accommodating, and get satisfaction from contributing to collective success rather than personal advancement.

Negative Implications

People with low scores on the Ambition scale seem unassertive and indecisive and may avoid taking the initiative. Satisfied with the status quo, they often lack career focus, identity, or vision. These people tend to not act unless asked to and may reject offers of leadership or advancement.

Table 4 contains the behavioral implications of low and high scores for Ambition. Table 5 contains definitions for Ambition's subscales (i.e., HICs) as well as interpretations for their low and high scores. If the assessed individual has a low or average Ambition score, the subscale scores become more important. Use them to help you interpret the Ambition score.

Table 4: Behavioral Implications of Ambition Scores

Low Ambition Score		High Ambition Score	
Positive Behaviors	Negative Behaviors	Positive Behaviors	Negative Behaviors
• Content with position in life • Compliant team player • Willing to follow others • Avoids office politics	• Lacks career focus or vision • Seems to lack energy • Avoids taking initiative • Uncomfortable making public presentations	• Energetic and competitive • Assertive and self-assured • Poised and leader-like • Unafraid to fail • Willing to take initiative • Sets high expectations • Goal- and results-oriented	• Too involved in office politics • Poor listener • Competes with others • May compete with team members • Pushy and impatient

Table 5: Ambition Subscales Interpretation

Ambition	Definition	Low Score	High Score
Competitive	Competitive, ambitious, and persistent	Laid-back	Competitive and determined to get ahead
Self-confident	Confidence in oneself	Lacking in confidence	Confident
Accomplishment	Goal attainment	Unhappy with accomplishments	Enjoyment of self and work
Leadership	Capacity for leadership	Reluctant to assume leadership responsibilities	Willing to assume positions of authority
Identity	Satisfaction with one's life tasks	Lacking in career direction	Focused career direction
No Social Anxiety	Social self-confidence	Socially retiring	Confident in social settings

Scale 3—Sociability

Sociability concerns the degree to which a person seems to need social contact and interaction. Key indicators include being talkative, socially bold, lively, approachable, and outgoing.

Performance Implications of High Scores (65%–100%)

Positive Implications

People with high scores on the Sociability scale are energetic, outgoing, and highly approachable. They feel very confident in social situations, easily initiate conversations with strangers, and can network for long periods. They do not feel embarrassed and seem to enjoy being the center of attention.

Negative Implications

People with high scores on the Sociability scale dominate conversations, interrupt others, and seem not to listen well. They compete for center stage, believing others find them interesting and attractive. They may also seem impulsive and make hasty decisions (check for a low Prudence score).

Performance Implications of Average Scores (36%–64%)

Positive Implications

People with average scores on the Sociability scale are approachable and balance listening with talking when interacting with others. These people are good at providing relevant feedback. They are also comfortable working alone or with others.

Negative Implications

People with average scores on the Sociability scale may struggle to find a balance between proactive and reactive communication. Their level of social engagement may depend on group size and result in inconsistencies in the ways they contribute to meetings or conversations.

Tips to consider:

- Those who score on the higher end of average scores seem congenial, approachable, and seek attention. They proactively communicate and tend to enjoy working with others more than working alone. These people may interrupt others and ignore their input.

- Those who score on the lower end of average scores are modest and slow to engage. They prefer to listen and may enjoy solitary tasks over collaboration. They do not make strong first impressions. They do not actively contribute during meetings and may be uncomfortable with strangers.

Performance Implications of Low Scores (0%–35%)

Positive Implications

People with low scores on the Sociability scale are reserved, independent, and comfortable working alone. They may seem remote, business focused, and task oriented. Good listeners, these people will not need continuous social stimulation to keep them interested and satisfied with their job.

Negative Implications

People with low scores on the Sociability scale may struggle to initiate conversations. They tend to be withdrawn and even seem cold or aloof (check the Reserved score). These people may avoid networking and fail to promote themselves effectively. As managers, they tend to hold back during discussions, seem unapproachable, and only give minimal feedback.

Table 6 contains the behavioral implications of low and high scores for Sociability. Table 7 contains definitions for Sociability's subscales (i.e., HICs) as well as interpretations for their low and high scores. If the assessed individual has a low or average Sociability score, the subscale scores become more important. Use them to help you interpret the Sociability score.

Table 6: Behavioral Implications of Sociability Scores

Low Sociability Score		High Sociability Score	
Positive Behaviors	**Negative Behaviors**	**Positive Behaviors**	**Negative Behaviors**
• Modest • Independent • Able to work on their own • Good listener • Strong relationships with a select few	• Uncomfortable meeting strangers • Dislikes giving others feedback • Does not network well • Social interactions are difficult and draining	• Outgoing and gregarious • Colorful • Talkative • Enjoys being the center of attention • Easily approachable • Enjoys working with others	• Dislikes working alone • Attention-seeking • Talks too much • May not listen well • Interrupts others • Impulsive and distractible

Table 7: Sociability Subscales Interpretations

Sociability	Definition	Low Score	High Score
Likes Parties	Enjoys parties	Not likely to enjoy social gatherings	Likely enjoys social gatherings
Likes Crowds	Finds large crowds exciting	Likely prefers smaller groups	Likely enjoys large groups
Experience Seeking	Prefers variety and new experiences	Unadventurous, prefers little variety	Adventurous, actively seeks out new experiences
Exhibitionistic	Exhibitionistic tendencies	Avoids the limelight	Attention-seeking
Entertaining	Being witty and entertaining	Not particularly entertaining	Charming, amusing, good sense of humor

Scale 4—Interpersonal Sensitivity

Interpersonal sensitivity concerns the degree to which a person seems perceptive, insightful, diplomatic, and socially sensitive. Key indicators include warmth, tact, charm, and skill at maintaining relationships.

Performance Implications of High Scores (65%–100%)

Positive Implications

People with high scores on the Interpersonal Sensitivity scale seem warm, tolerant, diplomatic, thoughtful, and considerate. They excel at building and maintaining relationships. They are socially insightful and easily navigate complex social situations. As managers, they encourage cooperation and teamwork, fostering trust and respect in their peers and staff.

Negative Implications

People with high scores on the Interpersonal Sensitivity scale may be overly concerned with pleasing others, potentially leading to difficulty in making tough decisions. Their strong desire for harmony can result in avoiding confrontations. They may seem reluctant to hold people accountable for their performance, creating possible perceptions of favoritism with direct reports.

Performance Implications of Average Scores (36%–64%)

Positive Implications

People with average scores on the Interpersonal Sensitivity scale are easygoing, tolerant, and considerate of others while also sharing direct, honest feedback when necessary. Their diplomatic skills allow them to address conflicts based on their audience. They tend to confront problems promptly and deliver what they promise.

Negative Implications

People with average scores on the Interpersonal Sensitivity scale may be inconsistent when trying to balance candor and tact. They may try to prioritize both relationships and productivity and fail on both accounts. Their diplomatic skills could falter, leading to miscommunications or conflicts.

Tips to consider:

- Those who score on the higher end of average scores appear to be pleasant, cooperative, and diplomatic. They are likely attuned to the feelings of others. However, they may seem averse to conflict and too eager to please.

- Those who score on the lower end of average scores tend to be candid, use a more direct style of communication, and are willing to take independent positions when appropriate. They will likely be quick to address conflict but may be impatient and criticize others.

Performance Implications of Low Scores (0%–35%)

Positive Implications

People with low scores on the Interpersonal Sensitivity scale are independent, direct, and transparent in their interactions. Their clear communication style can be beneficial in task-oriented environments. They are not afraid to take unpopular positions and defend them. They are also willing to give people negative feedback and hold them accountable for their performance.

Negative Implications

People with low scores on the Interpersonal Sensitivity scale tend to be abrupt, blunt, direct, and seem indifferent to the impact their remarks may have on others. They may seem impatient with poor performance and ready to criticize others.

Table 8 contains the behavioral implications of low and high scores for the Interpersonal Sensitivity scale. Table 9 contains definitions for Interpersonal Sensitivity's subscales (i.e., HICs) as well as interpretations for their low and high scores. If the assessed individual has a low or average Interpersonal Sensitivity score, the subscale scores become more important. Use them to help you interpret the Interpersonal Sensitivity score.

Table 8: Behavioral Implications of Interpersonal Sensitivity Scores

Low Sociability Score		High Sociability Score	
Positive Behaviors	Negative Behaviors	Positive Behaviors	Negative Behaviors
• Task oriented • Provides candid feedback • Speaks their mind • Forthright and independent • Challenges assumptions • Confronts others	• Can be blunt and unsympathetic • Critical and challenging • Tells rather than suggests • Can be stubborn • Not a good team player	• Warm and agreeable • Encourages cooperation and teamwork • Solicits opinions and feedback • Builds and maintains trust	• Thin-skinned and easily upset • Reluctant to disagree publicly with others • Conflict averse • Slow to make decisions • Avoids confronting performance problems

Table 9: Interpersonal Sensitivity Subscales Interpretation

Interpersonal Sensitivity	Definition	Low Score	High Score
Easy to Live With	Tolerant and easygoing nature	Not always tolerant and kindhearted	Likely to be perceived as easygoing
Sensitive	Tends to be kind and considerate	Not very tactful	Tactful
Caring	Shows concern for others	Unappreciative of others' needs	Perceptive and understanding
Likes People	Enjoys social interaction	Socially withdrawn	Likely to enjoy others' company
No Hostility	Lack of hostility	Critical of others	Generally accepting

Scale 5—Prudence

Prudence concerns the degree to which a person seems conscientious, conforming, and dependable. Key indicators include being planful, organized, socially appropriate, and hardworking.

Performance Implications of High Scores (65%–100%)

Positive Implications

People with high scores on the Prudence scale tend to be highly conscientious, reliable, organized, and respectful of authority (check the Dutiful score). They plan their work in advance, follow procedures, and respect rules. They are good role models and organizational citizens who make decisions carefully based on thorough reviews of the available information.

Negative Implications

People with high scores on the Prudence scale may struggle with flexibility, sometimes becoming overly cautious or rigid. They can become perfectionistic, possibly slowing decision-making and project progress. Others may describe them as inflexible, overly dependent on precedent, and reluctant to innovate.

Performance Implications of Average Scores (36%–64%)

Positive Implications

People with average scores on the Prudence scale are planful yet flexible. They adjust to change, strike a good balance between speed and accuracy, and delegate responsibly.

Negative Implications

People with average scores on the Prudence scale may inconsistently apply standards and rules. They may contradict themselves, potentially leading to misunderstandings or miscommunication. These people may not follow through on their planning endeavors and could overlook details if rushed.

Tips to consider:

- Those who score on the higher end of average scores appear to be responsible, respectful of hierarchy, and comfortable with close supervision. They may struggle with prioritizing work and changing circumstances.

- Those who score on the lower end of average scores may be more spontaneous, flexible, and tolerant of ambiguity. They may act in haste and ignore process steps if they do not personally find value in the procedure.

Performance Implications of Low Scores (0%–35%)

Positive Implications

People with low scores on the Prudence scale seem flexible, spontaneous, and adventurous. Taking risks and testing limits, they quickly adapt to new tasks or unexpected challenges. These people are usually open to innovation and comfortable questioning traditional methods, which can foster creativity and encourage others to think outside the box.

Negative Implications

People with low scores on the Prudence scale can be impulsive, disruptive, and careless about rules and procedures. They may resist close supervision and challenge authority. They can appear careless or indifferent to others, undermining trust or credibility.

Table 10 contains the behavioral implications of low and high scores for Prudence. Table 11 contains definitions for Prudence's subscales (i.e., HICs) as well as interpretations for their low and high scores. If the assessed individual has a low or average Prudence score, the subscale scores become more important. Use them to help you interpret the Prudence score.

Table 10: Behavioral Implications of Prudence scores

Low Prudence Score		High Prudence Score	
Positive Behaviors	**Negative Behaviors**	**Positive Behaviors**	**Negative Behaviors**
• Flexible • Adaptive • Open to change • Unafraid of risk • Welcomes innovation	• Tests limits unnecessarily • Careless and inattentive • Easily bored • Impulsive • Resists supervision	• Dependable and reliable • Rule following • Conscientious and hardworking • Good organizational citizen • Good with planning, implementation, and follow-through	• Resistant to change • Micromanages others • Does not delegate well • Unable to prioritize tasks • Inflexible about rules and procedures

Table 11: Prudence Subscales Interpretation

Prudence	Definition	Low Score	High Score
Moralistic	Adheres strictly to conventional values	Inclined to set own rules	Willing to follow rules
Mastery	Hardworking	Relaxed attitude about work	Concerned with doing a good job
Virtuous	Being principled	Willing to admit minor faults	Concerned with being upstanding and highly principled
Not Autonomous	Concerned about others' opinions	Independent and resistant to feedback	Concerned about others' perceptions
Not Spontaneous	Preference for predictability	Spontaneous	Planful in approach
Impulse Control	Lack of impulsivity	Impulsive	Cautious in approach
Avoids Trouble	Avoids unnecessary risks	Prone to unnecessary and negative risk-taking	Likely to anticipate consequences

Scale 6—Inquisitive

The Inquisitive scale concerns the degree to which a person seems open minded, innovative, and interested in ideas. Key indicators include being curious, imaginative, tolerant, and seeking stimulus; they may be easily bored.

Performance Implications of High Scores (65%–100%)

Positive Implications

People with high scores on the Inquisitive scale seem imaginative and insightful, with a wide range of interests. They are described as creative (check for a low Prudence score), curious, tolerant, open minded, and interested in ideas. They can be outside-the-box thinkers who bring a variety of different ideas and solutions to the table.

Negative Implications

People with high scores on the Inquisitive scale need stimulation and may be easily bored. They may seem impractical, be uninterested in operational or process matters, and prefer to think about strategy rather than implementation.

Performance Implications of Average Scores (36%–64%)

Positive Implications

People with average scores on the Inquisitive scale are practical problem-solvers. They can translate big ideas into actionable steps or a plan of action. These people can effectively balance innovation with operational tasks.

Negative Implications

People with average scores on the Inquisitive scale may struggle to balance innovation with execution, tending to get stuck in one mindset or the other. Torn between maintaining tradition and embracing change, they may struggle to generate new ideas.

Tips to consider:

- Those who score on the higher end of average scores can plan and translate visionary ideas into solutions. They may sometimes become too engaged with unrealistic projects, not recognizing when they need a more practical approach.

- Those who score on the lower end of average scores tend to take a hands-on, iterative approach to problem-solving. They may focus on details and operational matters, ignoring larger strategic concerns.

Performance Implications of Low Scores (0%–35%)

Positive Implications

People with low scores on the Inquisitive scale tend to be pragmatic, grounded, and comfortable with routine, established methods. They prefer predictable environments with consistent, clear guidelines that allow them to perform reliably and efficiently.

Negative Implications

People with low scores on the Inquisitive scale may struggle with ambiguity, novelty, or change, finding it difficult to adjust quickly to new circumstances or innovative approaches. They tend to focus on details and operational matters and ignore larger strategic concerns.

Table 12 contains the behavioral implications of low and high scores for Inquisitive. Table 13 contains definitions for Inquisitive's subscales (i.e., HICs) as well as interpretations for their low and high scores. If the assessed individual has a low or average Inquisitive score, the subscale scores become more important. Use them to help you interpret the Inquisitive score.

Table 12: Behavioral Implications of Inquisitive Scores

Low Inquisitive Score		High Inquisitive Score	
Positive Behaviors	**Negative Behaviors**	**Positive Behaviors**	**Negative Behaviors**
• Seldom questions rules and procedures • Focused interests • Enjoys routine tasks • Not easily bored • Can attend to the details of the business	• Lacks imagination • Resists innovation • Ignores the big picture • Uncomfortable with ambiguity • Has a tactical perspective	• Curious and imaginative • Tolerant • Understands the big picture • Open to change • Interested in new ideas • Thinks strategically about business	• Impractical • Overly inclusive thinking • Impatient with details • Dislikes routine • Easily bored • Poor implementation

Table 13: Inquisitive Subscales Interpretation

Inquisitive	Definition	Low Score	High Score
Science Ability	Interest in science	Little interest in why things happen	Strong interest in why things happen
Curiosity	Curiosity about the world	Low degree of curiosity	High degree of curiosity
Thrill Seeking	Enjoys adventure and excitement	No interest in challenge, stimulation, and excitement	Seeks challenge, stimulation, and excitement
Intellectual Games	Enjoys intellectual games	No interest in intellectual games	High interest in riddles and puzzles
Generates Ideas	Ideational fluency	Not good at generating ideas	Good at generating new ideas
Culture	Interest in culture	Narrow interests	Wide variety of cultural interests and activities

Scale 7—Learning Approach

The Learning Approach scale concerns the degree to which a person seems to enjoy learning and value education for its own sake. Key indicators include being analytical, clever, rational, and strategic.

Performance Implications of High Scores (65%–100%)

Positive Implications

People with high scores on the Learning Approach scale seem smart and well informed. They value education and see learning new material as something important for its own sake. These people work to stay up to date with current developments in their profession and strive to apply their knowledge to situations.

Negative Implications

People with high scores on the Learning Approach scale tend to value education without considering if it will directly improve job performance. They may adopt new technologies before evaluating their usefulness or applicability. These people often seem to want to show off their new knowledge, which can cause them to be seen as know-it-alls, thereby eroding their credibility.

Performance Implications of Average Scores (36%–64%)

Positive Implications

People with average scores on the Learning Approach scale enjoy learning and training that is applicable and addresses a direct need. They look for learning opportunities with clear connections to their roles and career. These people encourage others to learn new technology but only if they believe they have a strong use case.

Negative Implications

People with average scores on the Learning Approach scale may hesitate to seek learning opportunities beyond mandatory training. They may be complacent with their skills and need to be convinced of the need to upskill. These people may be slow to adapt to new or untested technology.

Tips to consider:

- Those who score on the higher end of average scores stay alert for learning opportunities and encourage others to remain up to date with those areas critical to their role or industry. They may fail to appraise the usefulness of technical solutions.

- Those who score on the lower end of average scores tend to be skeptical of unproved methods and technologies. They may see most traditional educational experiences as unnecessary unless directly related to their current needs and, thus, do not seize learning opportunities for their own career growth.

Performance Implications of Low Scores (0%–35%)

Positive Implications

People with low scores on the Learning Approach scale prefer to learn through experience and on-the-job training. They are practical, grounded, and interested in what works and are skeptical about adopting new technology that does not clearly impact job performance.

Negative Implications

People with low scores on Learning Approach view traditional educational experiences as something to be endured rather than something that may be helpful. Consequently, they often seem unconcerned with staff development and may not provide new skill development opportunities needed to improve staff's work. At risk of relying on inefficient, outdated methods and procedures, they may let helpful technology pass them by.

Table 14 contains the behavioral implications of low and high scores for Learning Approach. Table 15 contains definitions for Learning Approach's subscales (i.e., HICs) as well as interpretations for their low and high scores. If the assessed individual has a low or average Learning Approach score, the subscale scores become more important. Use them to help you interpret the Learning Approach score.

Table 14: Behavioral Implications of Learning Approach Scores

Low Learning Approach Score		High Learning Approach Score	
Positive Behaviors	**Negative Behaviors**	**Positive Behaviors**	**Negative Behaviors**
• Prefers learning on the job • Prefers practical training • Values functionality over the promises of new technology	• Endures education • May resist innovation • Unconcerned with staff development	• Enjoys and values education • Seems well-informed • Helps others learn • Stays up to date with developments in technology and business	• Impatient with those who are uninformed • May prefer training to working • May be a know-it-all • May lack depth on topics

Table 15: Learning Approach Subscales Interpretation

Learning Approach	Definition	Low Score	High Score
Education	Good student	Negative attitude about education	Positive attitude about education
Math Ability	Good with numbers	Weakness in working with numbers	Facility with numbers
Good Memory	Good memory	Somewhat forgetful	Good/accurate recall
Reading	Enjoys reading	Knowledge may be dated and not contemporary	Knowledge is likely current and up-to-date

Chapter 4
Hogan Development Survey

The Hogan Development Survey (HDS) assesses 11 patterns of interpersonal behavior that interfere with people's ability to develop productive relationships and prevent managers from building high-performing teams. The HPI concerns "filtered" behavior—how people behave when they are paying attention, for example, during a job interview. The HDS concerns "unfiltered" behavior—how people behave when they are not paying attention. Thus, the performance problems associated with the HDS primarily occur when people are not actively managing their public brand or image. This includes stressful situations as well as situations in which people are so comfortable that they stop attending to how they are seen.

Foundations of the HDS

Some background may help explain the meaning of the HDS. Sigmund Freud, Alfred Adler, Karen Horney, and H. S. Sullivan are famous psychiatrists who studied self-defeating behavior, but they explained self-defeating behavior in different ways. Freud was an *intrapsychic* theorist, whereas Adler, Horney, and Sullivan were *interpersonal* theorists. Freud studied unconscious thoughts operating inside people's minds, whereas the others studied the dynamics of social interaction. For Freud, how you think about yourself determines how you treat others. For the interpersonal theorists, how others treat you determines how you think about yourself. It is, of course, a matter of emphasis.

Freud thought everyone is more or less neurotic; the interpersonal theorists thought that most people have problems, but their problems are mostly not severe. Freud thought people could be characterized in terms of how they managed their neuroses; the interpersonal theorists thought people could be characterized by how they expected to be treated by others. Because some people's expectations are wrong, they tend to behave in ways that disrupt relationships and interfere with life goals.

Freud's view that everyone is neurotic is surely incorrect—people who are neurotic are deeply disturbed, and most people are not deeply disturbed. Nonetheless, among psychologists, Freud's view prevailed and determined the early history of personality measurement—specifically, the development of the Minnesota Multiphasic Personality Inventory (MMPI; Hathaway & McKinley, 1943; and the MMPI 2; Butcher et al., 1989), one of the best-known inventories in the history of personality assessment.

The interpersonal theorists argue that most people are not neurotic, but childhood experiences lead almost everyone to feel inadequate about something. That is, childhood is usually problematic in certain ways, and most people develop expectations about being criticized in certain situations while also developing methods for dealing with that criticism. For Freud, all neuroses have the same cause—a failure to resolve the Oedipus complex. For the interpersonal theorists, people feel inadequate for different reasons; almost everyone feels insecure about something—few people have perfect childhoods.

Interpersonal theorists have had a much smaller influence on personality assessment than Freud, despite the importance of the problems they studied. Other than research on Leary's interpersonal circumplex (Wiggins, 1979), there has been little systematic effort to classify the key interpersonal processes. To begin studying these processes, we need a taxonomy, a catalogue of the main themes associated with flawed interpersonal behavior. Horney (1950) identified 10 "neurotic needs," becoming one of the first taxonomies of flawed interpersonal tendencies. She summarized these neurotic needs in terms of three themes:

- Moving away from people—Managing one's feelings of inadequacy by avoiding contact with others

- Moving against people—Managing one's self-doubts by dominating and intimidating others

- Moving toward people—Managing one's insecurities by building alliances

We believe that Horney's taxonomy is a useful first step in classifying performance risks; moreover, her taxonomy is implicit in the classification of personality disorders originally contained in the *Diagnostic and Statistical Manual of Mental Disorders, Fourth Edition* (*DSM-IV*; American Psychiatric Association, 1994).

Development Guidelines

We developed the HDS based on four considerations. The first was what to include. The personality disorders, as described in the *DSM* series, provide a taxonomy of flawed interpersonal strategies that exist in the range of normal personality. Table 16 presents the 11 HDS scales with their performance risks compared with the personality disorders they parallel.

Table 16: Evolution of the Hogan Development Survey

DSM–IV, Axis 2		HDS	
Labels	**Theme**	**Scale**	**Theme**
Borderline	Inappropriate anger; unstable and intense relationships alternating between idealization and devaluation	Excitable	Moody and hard to please; intense, but short-lived enthusiasm for people, projects, or things
Paranoid	Distrustful and suspicious of others; motives are interpreted as malevolent	Skeptical	Cynical, distrustful, and doubting others' true intentions
Avoidant	Social inhibition; feelings of inadequacy and hypersensitivity to criticism or rejection	Cautious	Reluctant to take risks for fear of being rejected or negatively evaluated
Schizoid	Emotional coldness and detachment from social relationships; indifferent to praise and criticism	Reserved	Aloof, detached, and uncommunicative; lacking interest in or awareness of the feelings of others
Passive-Aggressive	Passive resistance to adequate social and occupational performance; irritated when asked to do something he/she does not want to do	Leisurely	Independent; ignoring people's requests and becoming irritated or argumentative if they persist
Narcissistic	Arrogant and haughty behaviors or attitudes; grandiose sense of self-importance and entitlement	Bold	Unusually self-confident; feelings of grandiosity and entitlement; overevaluation of one's capabilities
Antisocial	Disregard for the truth; impulsivity and failure to plan ahead; failure to conform with social norms	Mischievous	Enjoys taking risks and testing limits; needs excitement; manipulative, deceitful, cunning, and exploitative
Histrionic	Excessive emotionality and attention-seeking; self-dramatizing, theatrical, and exaggerated emotional expression	Colorful	Expressive, animated, and dramatic; wanting to be noticed and to be the center of attention
Schizotypal	Odd beliefs or magical thinking; behavior or speech that is odd, eccentric, or peculiar	Imaginative	Acting and thinking in creative and sometimes odd or unusual ways

Table 16 (continued): Evolution of the Hogan Development Survey

DSM–IV, Axis 2		HDS	
Labels	Theme	Scale	Theme
Obsessive-Compulsive	Preoccupations with orderliness, rules, perfectionism, and control; overly conscientious and inflexible	Diligent	Meticulous, precise, and perfectionistic; inflexible about rules and procedures; critical of others' performance
Dependent	Difficulty making everyday decisions without excessive advice and reassurance; difficulty expressing disagreement out of fear of loss of support or approval	Dutiful	Eager to please and reliant on others for support and guidance; reluctant to take independent action or go against popular opinion

The second consideration was how to conceptualize the constructs listed in Table 16. Many people define personality disorders as types, whereby each type refers to a distinct cluster of behaviors that characterize certain people. In our view, however, the performance risks assessed by the HDS are dimensional. People are normally distributed on these dimensions, and any single person may have high or low scores on any of the dimensions.

The third consideration for developing the HDS was how to assess the various personality disorders. The standard approach is to write items for each personality disorder using the diagnostic criteria listed in the *DSM-IV*. For example, the criteria for the Avoidant personality include sensitivity to criticism, prone to anxiety, fearfulness, and low self-confidence. To develop an Avoidant scale, therefore, a test author would write items reflecting each of these themes. The problem is that the *DSM-IV* assigns many of the same attributes to more than one personality disorder. For example, being sensitive to criticism is a criterion for diagnosing 4 of the 10 standard disorders, and items concerning being sensitive to criticism would appear on four different scales constructed in this manner. This builds in item overlap, necessarily reducing the power of such inventories to discriminate among people.

To avoid this problem, we wrote HDS items directed at the heart of each tendency and then carefully reviewed the item content across scales to eliminate item overlap, enhancing the entire inventory's discriminatory power. Thus, for example, items on the Skeptical scale concern suspiciousness, mistrust, and a heightened readiness to confront people suspected of betrayal, whereas items on the Reserved scale concern being aloof, insensitive, and indifferent to the problems of others. The content of each scale is independent of the content of the other scales.

The final consideration that shaped the development of the HDS was the actual item content. The HDS is intended to be used in everyday contexts for career and leadership development, job placement, promotion, and other talent management decisions. This contrasts with inventories designed to determine mental health status or to be used for medical evaluations. Our items reflect themes from the world of work (e.g., how one relates to supervisors, coworkers, and friends; attitudes toward competition and success). In addition, the scales have been labeled so that people receiving high scores on the various dimensions are not stigmatized. Finally, we are aware of the implications of recent rulings, especially the Americans with Disabilities Act of 1990 (ADA, 1990, as amended) and *Karraker v. Rent-A-Center, Inc.* (2005), as they affect test item content (Hogan et al., 1996; Winterberg et al., 2019). The items on the HDS have been carefully reviewed to ensure they do not contain medical or psychiatric content. Furthermore, as part of our Kaizen Psychometrics process, we continuously update item content to ensure the HDS complies with all legal requirements.

Initial Development

The original model for the HDS was PROFILE, developed by Warren Jones (1988) shortly after the *DSM-III*, Axis 2 personality disorders (American Psychiatric Association, 1987) appeared. Jones developed PROFILE as an alternative to the personality disorder inventories available at the time. We conducted several validity studies using PROFILE and found that it reliably predicted poor job performance. We concluded that assessing "performance risks" in the workplace was needed. However, we were concerned about the PROFILE's emphasis on anxiety and depression. With the passage of the ADA (1990), we thought the PROFILE would be seen as evaluating mental disabilities, something prohibited in pre-offer employment inquiries.

Our strategy for writing items for the HDS focused on the distinctive characteristics of each performance risk. We wrote items with work-related and interpersonal content, avoiding items referring to clinical or medical themes, religious beliefs, or sexual preferences. Like the HPI, the HDS items are designed to reflect what a person with a particular performance risk might say or do.

Finally, trying to develop scales that did not overlap and had homogeneous themes, we avoided repeating descriptors across scales. This was challenging because symptoms such as anxiety are common to many standard personality disorders. We also tried to minimize correlations between the scales.

We began working on the HDS in the fall of 1992. We wrote an initial set of items, tested them with samples of people, computed internal consistency reliability statistics and correlations with other well-established measures, reviewed the data, and revised the items to (a) enhance internal consistency reliability and (b) sharpen convergent and discriminant validity. We also received valuable input from many colleagues in the United States and Europe about the scales' content. The HDS is the product of six cycles of item writing, revision, testing, and further revision, with the final set of items being defined during the summer of 1995. From 1995 to 1996, we assessed more than 2,000 people, including employed adults, job applicants, prisoners, and graduate students, ranging in age from 21 years to 64 years, with a mean of 38.5 years. There were 1,532 men and 322 women, with 620 identifying as White and 150 identifying as Black. We estimate that about 15% of the sample were college educated.

Later Development

The HDS is designed to predict behavioral tendencies that can impede or "derail" career success. Considerable evidence shows that these tendencies are commonplace. For example, Bentz (1985) identified themes associated with managerial failure (e.g., playing politics, being moody and dishonest) in the retail industry. Researchers at the Center for Creative Leadership and at Personnel Decisions International have previously reported that technically competent managers who fail seem arrogant, vindictive, untrustworthy, selfish, emotional, compulsive, overly controlling, insensitive, abrasive, aloof, too ambitious, or unable to delegate (Hazucha, 1991; Lombardo et al., 1988; McCall & Lombardo, 1983). The performance risks assessed by the HDS reflect common themes in the lives of people who are getting by but perhaps gradually failing or at least not realizing their potential.

More than 4 million employed adults representing every sector of the global marketplace, including manufacturing, communications, health care, retail, banking and finance, construction, transportation, security, law enforcement, and many others have taken the HDS. We have conducted more than 100 validation studies covering a wide range of job categories. Most of these studies link HDS scores with ratings of managerial/professional incompetence and show that the inventory accounts for unique variance beyond that obtained with traditional inventories of normal personality.

HDS scores are stable over time, with test–retest reliabilities ranging from .60 to .75 (mean = .69). Although individual scores are stable, we believe that focused development efforts can reduce the effects of high scores. Put another way, people who are aware of their high HDS scores can take action to mitigate the likelihood of negative behaviors on the job. This is the foundation for using the HDS in dozens of development programs. Many of these programs improve leaders' performances by helping them eliminate or reduce the negative behaviors highlighted by the HDS.

Summary of the Current Structure of the HDS

The scales of the HDS reflect people's flawed beliefs about how to deal with other people; these tendencies can be grouped into three broad categories:

- Moving Away—These behaviors involve managing social interaction by maintaining social distance and pushing others away.

- Moving Against—These behaviors involve managing social interaction by manipulating and controlling others.

- Moving Toward—These behaviors involve managing social interaction by keeping others close.

Extreme (very high or very low) HPI scores can have potentially negative consequences that resemble the tendencies predicted by the HDS. However, the HPI and the HDS are not redundant. Each provides unique insights into one's tendencies for a more complete understanding.

HDS HICs

Two separate lines of inquiry led to developing the HDS's subscale structure. First, years of interpreting HDS results led us to recognize predictable behavioral themes associated with each of the 11 primary scales. Second, clients began asking for more detailed information for each HDS scale. These observations signaled a need to review each HDS scale to identify subscales represented by behavioral themes. We identified and validated three subscales for each HDS scale. In 2014, we added 33 subscales (i.e., HICs) to the HDS.

General Interpretive Guidelines for the HDS

- The HDS can be used for selection with appropriate validation data and for individual development (particularly for people in or aspiring to leadership positions).

- Interpreting HDS results is not job specific. The counterproductive behaviors associated with high or low scores are likely to appear whenever people are not paying attention to their public image.

- High and low HDS scores are associated with both positive and negative behaviors. There is good news and bad news at both ends of the scales.

- For the sake of convenience, we define scores between 0% and 39% as "no risk," between 40% and 69% as "low risk," between 70% and 89% as "moderate risk," and above 90% as "high risk."

- It is important to stress that these categories of no risk, low risk, moderate risk, and high risk are arbitrary distinctions.

- Scores between 0% and 10% and scores between 90% and 100% are especially informative and strongly indicative of behavioral tendencies.

- On average, individuals have 3.7 HDS scores in the moderate-risk or high-risk categories. If a person has four or more moderate-risk or high-risk scores, then their behavior is likely to be more problematic. If a person has no high-risk or no-risk scores, then this person's low- and moderate-risk scores become more meaningful.

HDS Global Portability

Our data show that the HDS predicts behavior that impedes job performance and career success across cultures and languages—that is, the performance risks assessed by the HDS resonate as well in the international marketplace as they do domestically. As with the HPI, we have engaged in large-scale translation efforts. At the time of this printing, the HDS is available online in the following languages:

- Arabic
- Azerbaijani
- Bulgarian
- Chinese (Simplified)
- Chinese (Traditional)
- Croatian
- Czech
- Danish
- Dutch
- English (Australian and New Zealand)
- English (Greek)
- English (Indian)
- English (Kenyan)
- English (Middle Eastern)
- English (South African)
- English (UK)
- English (US)
- Estonian
- Finnish
- French (Canadian)
- French (Parisian)
- German
- Greek
- Hebrew
- Hungarian
- Icelandic
- Indonesian
- Italian

- Japanese
- Korean
- Latvian
- Macedonian
- Malaysian
- Montenegrin
- Norwegian
- Polish
- Portuguese (Brazilian)
- Portuguese (European)
- Romanian
- Russian
- Serbian
- Slovak
- Slovenian
- Spanish (Castilian)
- Spanish (Latin American)
- Swedish
- Thai
- Turkish
- Ukrainian
- Vietnamese

As with the HPI, we are also expanding our norm data and validation research throughout the global marketplace for the HDS. The HDS's to-date norms and validity results continue to support its global portability.

Chapter 5

How to Interpret the Hogan Development Survey

Scale 1—Excitable

The Excitable scale concerns behaviors ranging from an unemotional, passive acceptance of life to an intense and emotionally explosive engagement with life. People with high scores for the Excitable scale tend to have strong and passionate involvements in projects or people; over time, however, they become disappointed, give up, and have terminal breaks. They also tend to catastrophize when other people disappoint them or projects seem to go wrong. Consequently, people with high scores may seem to lack persistence.

The following behaviors are typically associated with moderate to high risk scores:

- Ready to give up when things go wrong

- Easily upset and hard to soothe

- Overly sensitive to feedback

- Moody and emotionally unpredictable

Performance Implications of High Risk Scores (90%–100%)

People with High Risk scores seem intense, passionate, and driven, but also edgy, volatile, and explosive. They tend to develop strong enthusiasm for people, projects, or organizations; over time, they may become disappointed and lose their passion. When they become disappointed, they often give up and abandon their commitments. They tend to be easily annoyed, they let little things bother them, and they change jobs more frequently than other people. Although they bring considerable energy and enthusiasm to projects, they may be hard to work with because they seem moody, easily upset, and emotionally unpredictable.

Performance Implications of Moderate Risk Scores (70%–89%)

Individuals with Moderate Risk scores seem energetic and engaged with projects and people, but also moody and irritable. When provoked, they tend to overreact, and when projects do not go well, they tend to give up. They can bring helpful energy to new projects, but working with them may be challenging because they seem temperamental and overly sensitive to criticism.

Performance Implications of Low Risk Scores (40%–69%)

People with Low Risk scores seem calm and even-tempered. They are usually steady and tend not to overreact to frustration and stress. They are unlikely to need reassurance and usually tolerate others' shortcomings. These people tend to remain calm in emergencies. Those who score at the higher end of this range may display more intense emotions. Those who score at the lower end may lack energy and a sense of urgency.

Performance Implications of No Risk Scores (0%–39%)

People with No Risk scores seem calm, steady, composed, and emotionally stable. They are usually in a good mood, are not easily disappointed or frustrated, and maturely express their emotions. They may also seem somewhat detached, unconcerned, untroubled, and lacking energy and a sense of urgency.

Table 17 contains definitions for Excitable's subscales.

Table 17: Excitable Subscales

Subscale	Definition
Volatile	Moody, often angered or annoyed, easily upset and hard to soothe
Easily Disappointed	Initial passion for people and projects that inevitably disappoint, and passion then turns to rejection
No Direction	Lacking few well-defined beliefs or interests but with regrets about past behavior

Scale 2—Skeptical

The Skeptical scale concerns behaviors ranging from trusting and believing in others to expecting malintent or to be mistreated. High scorers tend to be insightful about interpersonal and organizational politics but can be cynical and mistrustful and take negative feedback personally. People with high scores also seem quarrelsome and likely to hold grudges, possibly for a long time.

The following behaviors are typically associated with Moderate to High Risk scores:

- Insightful about people and organizational politics

- Argumentative

- Defensive and resistant to feedback

- Suspicious of others' intentions

- Willing to retaliate when they feel wronged

Performance Implications of High Risk Scores (90%–100%)

People with High Risk scores seem smart and insightful and often have well-developed, complicated theories about politics and society. They also seem critical, find faults in others, and are alert for signs of betrayal. They tend to be perceptive but cynical, easily angered, vengeful, and expecting to be mistreated. Although they are shrewd and difficult to fool, they are often hard to work with because they tend to be argumentative and disputatious, often retaliating when they feel wronged.

Performance Implications of Moderate Risk Scores (70%–89%)

People with Moderate Risk scores seem insightful about others' motives, but skeptical and critical. When they do not understand why they should do something, they can be uncooperative. Others tend to see them as defensive, thin-skinned, argumentative, and suspicious of authority. They may be challenging to work with because they tend to exaggerate grievances, feel misused, and withdraw when they feel wronged.

Performance Implications of Low Risk Scores (40%–69%)

People with Low Risk scores seem tolerant, trusting, fair minded, and possibly naïve. They likely have a realistic view of organizational politics and seem cooperative. They tend to build stable, long-term relationships and willingly accept feedback and criticism without becoming defensive. They tend not to hold grudges, usually trust others, and are easy to coach. Those who score on the higher end of the range may display cynicism and require more time to extend their trust. Those who score on the lower end of the range may be too trusting and naïve.

Performance Implications of No Risk Scores (0%–39%)

People with No Risk scores seem optimistic, positive, trusting, and sometimes naïve. They are open to feedback and do not take criticism personally. They tend to believe in others and in giving them second chances—they are willing to forgive and forget; consequently, they tend to form long-term relationships while seeming trusting and possibly gullible.

Table 18 contains definitions for Skeptical's subscales.

Table 18: Skeptical Subscales

Subscale	Definition
Cynical	Prone to doubt others' intentions and assume they have bad ulterior motives
Mistrusting	Generalized mistrust of people and institutions, being alert for signs of perceived mistreatment
Grudges	Holding grudges and being unwilling to forgive real or perceived wrongs

Scale 3—Cautious

The Cautious scale concerns behaviors ranging from a confident willingness to undertake new ventures to being reluctant to take risks and try new things. High scorers seem to be preoccupied with avoiding criticism. Consequently, people with high scores may seem resistant to change and unwilling to take chances.

The following behaviors are typically associated with Moderate to High Risk scores:

- Slow decision-making

- Resistance to change

- Reluctance to take chances

- Fear of failure

- Being unassertive

- Perceived as overly controlling of subordinates

Performance Implications of High Risk Scores (90%–100%)

People with High Risk scores seem hesitant, conventional, restrained, and unassertive. They tend to avoid making decisions and are slow to adopt new procedures or technology because of the possibility of being criticized or embarrassed. They are good organizational citizens who follow company policies carefully and rarely make thoughtless decisions. They may be challenging to work with because they are indecisive and reluctant to take strong stances on issues or adopt new technologies. These people worry about making mistakes and may avoid difficult assignments.

Performance Implications of Moderate Risk Scores (70%–89%)

Individuals with Moderate Risk scores tend to be perceived as inhibited, careful, and indecisive. They can seem slow to make decisions or act, reluctant to try new methods, resistant to changes in policies and procedures, and may need extra support when faced with challenging assignments. Although they are usually good corporate citizens, others may find them hard to work with because they seem insecure, resistant to innovation or new procedures, and reluctant to take a stand on issues.

Performance Implications of Low Risk Scores (40%–69%)

People with Low Risk scores tend to be confident, decisive, and willing to experiment and accept new challenges. They usually evaluate risk appropriately, handle disappointments maturely, and seem open to innovations in policies and procedures. They seem willing to take a position on issues and then review the impact of their decisions. Those who score on the higher end of the range may be slower to make decisions or hesitate to speak up. Those who score on the lower range may seem too confident in their opinions or quick to make decisions.

Performance Implications of No Risk Scores (0%–39%)

People with No Risk scores seem to seek risk, be confident, and be unafraid of taking chances. They are decisive, willing to make mistakes, and open to innovation and difficult challenges. They are willing to take strong positions on complex issues and stand by them. However, they may be too confident in making decisions that involve considerable risk. They may not learn from their mistakes.

Table 19 contains definitions for Cautious's subscales.

Table 19: Cautious Subscales

Subscale	Definition
Avoidant	Avoiding new people and situations to prevent potential embarrassment
Fearful	Afraid of being criticized for making mistakes and being reluctant to act independently or make decisions
Unassertive	Unwilling to act assertively and therefore prone to being overlooked or ignored

Scale 4—Reserved

The Reserved scale concerns behaviors ranging from seeming sensitive to the feelings, reactions, and problems of others at one end, to seeming indifferent to, or unconcerned about, others' reactions at the other. The core of this dimension is the degree to which people seem concerned about how they impact others. People with low scores seem softhearted and caring; people with high scores seem tough, remote, and uncommunicative.

The following behaviors are typically associated with Moderate to High Risk scores:

- Blunt and insensitive

- Remote and uncommunicative

- Tough when under pressure

- Impassive and hard to read

- Obstinate and unbending

- Indifferent to criticism and feedback

Performance Implications of High Risk Scores (90%–100%)

People with High Risk scores seem tough, insensitive, self-directed, remote, and indifferent to feedback or criticism. They tend to avoid even minimal self-disclosure, prefer to work alone, and communicate in writing. They seem indifferent to the moods and feelings of others and/or how their actions impact them. They often communicate poorly, seem to ignore social cues or office politics, and rarely display support for their employers or coworkers. They handle stress, pressure, and criticism very well, and are steady in crises. Nonetheless, others may find working with them hard because they are aloof, uncommunicative, and unconcerned with the personal problems of others.

Performance Implications of Moderate Risk Scores (70%–89%)

People with Moderate Risk scores seem independent, tough, and detached. They tend to be formal with strangers and prefer to work alone. They may not communicate well and seem indifferent to issues of staff morale. Although these people may work well by themselves and easily handle stress, pressure, and bad news, others may find them difficult. This is because they tend to act without consulting others and only listen if they have a special interest in the message. These people handle criticism with ease and misinterpret feedback.

Performance Implications of Low Risk Scores (40%–69%)

People with Low Risk scores seem insightful and concerned about how they impact others. They seem able to read people and try to understand the perspectives of others. Those who score on the higher end of the range tend to be independent and sometimes insensitive. Those who score on the lower end of the range may be good team players but tend to be sensitive to feedback and criticism. As managers, they may be reluctant to have hard conversations and hold staff accountable for their performance.

Performance Implications of No Risk Scores (0%–39%)

People with No Risk scores seem empathic, kind, and understanding. They care about how they impact others, seem comfortable working with a variety of clients, and enjoy working on teams. They seem insightful about interpersonal issues, and sympathetic to others' feelings; they put people around them at ease. At the same time, they may be too sensitive to criticism. They are also likely to be conflict averse and unwilling to have difficult conversations and confront poor performance.

Table 20 contains definitions for Reserved's subscales.

Table 20: Reserved Subscales

Subscale	Definition
Introverted	Valuing one's private time and preferring to work alone
Unsocial	Keeping others at a distance, limiting close relationships, and being generally detached
Tough	Indifferent to the feelings and problems of others, focused on tasks rather than people

Scale 5—Leisurely

The Leisurely scale concerns being cynical about the competency of authority figures in organizations but unwilling to defy them. High scorers seem cooperative and compliant but are privately stubborn and uncooperative. They are socially skilled, insightful, and diplomatic, but they also seem indecisive, procrastinate, and often do not communicate clearly. Low scorers are more transparent, overtly defiant, and insubordinate.

The following behaviors are typically associated with Moderate to High Risk scores:

- Communicating in ways that avoid real commitment

- Indifferent to others' deadlines

- Overtly agreeable but covertly defiant

- Always saying yes but never saying when

- Procrastination

- Defiant in deniable ways, especially when assigned uninteresting work

Performance Implications of High Risk Scores (90%–100%)

People with high scores seem cooperative, pleasant, and diplomatic. Despite their surface agreeableness, they are suspicious of authority, work according to their own timetables, dislike being interrupted, and put off tasks they do not think are important. They are overtly charming but covertly independent and impertinent. They resent others' demands and privately question the competence of their bosses and coworkers. Although they seem pleasant and agreeable, others may find working with them challenging because they procrastinate, are stubborn, are reluctant to be part of a team, and tend not to follow through on commitments.

Performance Implications of Moderate Risk Scores (70%–89%)

People with Moderate Risk scores seem overtly pleasant, agreeable, and cooperative but privately tend to be stubborn and independent. They tend to procrastinate on, or resist, assigned tasks while offering plausible reasons for their lack of action. Although they typically have good social skills, they may be difficult to work with because they tend to put off unwanted tasks, question the competence of others, and choose which commitments they will honor.

Performance Implications of Low Risk Scores (40%–69%)

People with Low Risk scores seem open, direct, and candid. They are transparent and straightforward when communicating and/or dealing with others. They tend to follow through on their commitments or communicate when they cannot accept a request. Those on the higher end of the range may be subtle when they disagree. Those who score on the lower end may seem blunt, direct, and politically incorrect. These people respond well to coaching.

Performance Implications of No Risk Scores (0%–39%)

People with No Risk scores seem candid, direct, and transparent, and usually speak plainly, even to the point of being blunt (check for a low Interpersonal Sensitivity score). They willingly seek feedback and suggestions. These people tend to support their coworkers and to have few private agendas. At the same time, their social skills may seem somewhat undeveloped, and they can lack tact or timing when sharing their perspective.

Table 21 contains definitions for Leisurely's subscales.

Table 21: Leisurely Subscales

Subscale	Definition
Passive Aggressive	Overtly pleasant and compliant but privately resentful and subversive regarding requests for improved performance
Unappreciated	Believing that one's talents and contributions are ignored, perceiving inequities in assigned workloads
Irritated	Privately but easily irritated by interruptions, requests, or work-related suggestions

Scale 6—Bold

The Bold scale concerns behaviors ranging from humility and modest self-restraint to assertive self-promotion and dreams of success and power.

Important areas of concern include exaggerated views of one's competency and self-worth. People with high scores seem charismatic, confident, entitled, and unable to admit mistakes or learn from experience.

The following behaviors are typically associated with Moderate to High Risk scores:

- Resistance to feedback

- Overly confident in one's talent and capabilities

- Demanding and overbearing

- Prone to blaming others for their mistakes

- Self-promoting

- Entitled to respect, power, and compensation

- Self-centered and a poor team player

Performance Implications of High Risk Scores (90%–100%)

People with High Risk scores seem adventurous, energetic, ambitious, and forward looking. However, they may also be seen as impulsive, self-promoting, and demanding. They tend to overestimate their talents and accomplishments, ignore their shortcomings, and blame others for their mistakes. They typically make a strong first impression, but they can be hard to work with because they ignore feedback, test limits, intimidate others (especially subordinates), and feel entitled to leadership positions. As managers, they have trouble developing a sense of loyalty or teamwork among their associates.

Performance Implications of Moderate Risk Scores (70%–89%)

People with Moderate Risk scores seem energetic, confident, socially skilled, and unafraid of failure or rejection. They have challenging career goals, are willing to take initiative, and seek leadership positions. Although they tend to be charismatic and make strong first impressions, others may find them a challenge to work with because they tend to be demanding, entitled, and unwilling to acknowledge their mistakes or accept suggestions.

Performance Implications of Low Risk Scores (40%–69%)

People with Low Risk scores seem calm, understated, and easygoing, sometimes quiet. They seem tolerant, take direction well, and are willing to let others lead. Those who score on the higher end of the range tend to be confident in their abilities, have realistic career goals, but may overestimate themselves at times. Those who score on the lower end of the range tend not to seek public recognition (check for a low Recognition score) or speak up in meetings. As a result, they may be overlooked for advancement.

Performance Implications of No Risk Scores (0%–39%)

People with No Risk scores seem unassertive, content, modest, and humble. They seldom interrupt, criticize, test limits, or challenge others. They work well as part of a team, prefer to follow rather than lead, and rarely call attention to their accomplishments; as a result, their efforts may go unnoticed, and they may be overlooked for advancement.

Table 22 contains definitions for Bold's subscales.

Table 22: Bold Subscales

Subscale	Definition
Entitled	Feeling that one has special gifts and accomplishments and, consequently, deserves special treatment
Overconfidence	Unusually confident in one's abilities; belief that one will succeed at anything one chooses to undertake
Fantasized Talent	Believing that one has unusual talents and gifts and that one has been born for greatness

Scale 7—Mischievous

The Mischievous scale concerns behaviors ranging from seeming careful, quiet, conforming, and responsible to seeming bright, charming, impulsive, and limit testing. Important areas of concern include being careless about obligations, risk-taking, and excitement-seeking. People with high scores may have trouble meeting commitments and learning from experience.

The following behaviors are typically associated with Moderate to High Risk scores:

- Charming, impulsive, and daring

- Careless about established rules

- Unable to learn from mistakes

- Takes risks without reviewing consequences

- Enjoys testing limits

- Ignores commitments

Performance Implications of High Risk Scores (90%–100%)

People with High Risk scores seem bright, charming, daring, and unpredictable. They enjoy testing limits, seeking variety and excitement, and are easily bored. Although they often have strategic agendas, they are risk-seeking and may make impulsive decisions. They often seem not to care about disappointing others—because they expect to be forgiven. They are socially skilled and typically make favorable first impressions, but others may find them hard to work with because they tend to forget commitments, ignore their failures and mistakes, follow personal agendas, and rarely evaluate the consequences of their actions.

Performance Implications of Moderate Risk Scores (70%–89%)

People with Moderate Risk scores seem charming and impulsive and seek variety and adventure. They make decisions quickly, are unafraid of risk, and do not dwell on their mistakes. They seek variety and change and get easily bored. Although they are charming and entertaining, others may find working with them difficult because they test limits, are easily bored, and can be manipulative, tending to follow their personal agenda.

Performance Implications of Low Risk Scores (40%–69%)

People with Low Risk scores seem dependable, focused, and comfortable following standard rules and procedures. They are steady, predictable, likely to deliver on their commitments, and avoid taking unnecessary risks. Those who score on the higher end of the range tend to be more comfortable with risk and may ignore rules. Those who score on the lower end of the range may seem risk avoidant and are careful when making decisions.

Performance Implications of No Risk Scores (0%–39%)

People with No Risk scores seem compliant, responsible, and socially appropriate. They are self-controlled, reliable, and tend to make sound decisions. They avoid taking unnecessary risks, and others usually trust them, in part, because they think about the consequences of their decisions before acting. Unsurprisingly, they are rarely the life of the party. They may seem to avoid taking risks, even when necessary, and could be seen as slow to make decisions (check for a low Cautious score).

Table 23 contains definitions for Mischievous's subscales.

Table 23: Mischievous Subscales

Subscale	Definition
Risky	Prone to taking risks and testing limits, deliberately bending or breaking inconvenient rules
Impulsive	Tending to act impulsively without considering the long-term consequences of one's actions
Manipulative	Machiavellian tendencies—using charm to manipulate others with no remorse about doing so

Scale 8—Colorful

The Colorful scale concerns behaviors that range from modest self-restraint to excessive self-display. Important areas of concern include being boastful, socially distracting, and attention-seeking. People with high scores seem talkative, dramatic, and skilled at engaging and entertaining others.

The following behaviors are typically associated with Moderate to High Risk scores:

- Good at attracting attention to themselves

- Enjoys crises and the subsequent drama

- Confuses activity with productivity

- A poor listener

- Disorganized and lacks follow-through

Performance Implications of High Risk Scores (90%–100%)

People with High Risk scores seem outgoing, entertaining, socially skilled, and boastful. They seek high-profile positions, enjoy the limelight, network well, and are skilled at exercising influence. They tend to multitask and may have trouble staying on schedule, making decisions for the long term, and following through. They love having their accomplishments recognized and are clever at being noticed (e.g., making dramatic entrances and exits). They are energetic and entertaining, but others may find working with them difficult because they tend to be attention-seeking, overcommitted, distractible, and socially dominating.

Performance Implications of Moderate Risk Scores (70%–89%)

People with Moderate Risk scores seem interesting, entertaining, and lively. They make strong first impressions, enjoy high-profile positions, and expect others will find them entertaining. They are charming, engaging, and enjoy the limelight. Although they may be good company, others may find them hard to work with because they can be distracted, disorganized, unpredictable, and speaking more than they listen.

Performance Implications of Low Risk Scores (40%–69%)

People with Low Risk scores seem unpretentious, restrained, and socially balanced. They are usually willing to share credit, do not crave the limelight, and work well in supporting positions. Those who score on the higher end of the range tend to be talkative and may dominate conversations. Those who score on the lower end of the range seem self-controlled, but they may lack interpersonal energy.

Performance Implications of No Risk Scores (0%–39%)

People with No Risk scores seem modest, quiet, obliging, and self-restrained. They are responsible and dependable, willing to share credit, and may prefer to let others take the lead. They are most comfortable in roles "behind the scenes," and their natural modesty may cause bosses to overlook their other talents.

Table 24 contains definitions for Colorful's subscales.

Table 24: Colorful Subscales

Subscale	Definition
Public Confidence	Expecting others to find one's public performances fascinating and not knowing when to be quiet
Distractable	Easily distracted, minimal focus, needing constant stimulation, confusing activity with productivity
Self-Display	Wanting to be the center of attention and using dramatic costumes and gestures to attract attention to oneself

Scale 9—Imaginative

The Imaginative scale concerns behaviors ranging from seeming practical, sensible, and levelheaded to seeming unconventional, impractical, and wildly visionary. Important areas of concern include thinking and acting in impractical, arresting, creative, and even eccentric ways. People with high scores may appear visionary and innovative but may lack sound judgment.

The following behaviors are typically associated with Moderate to High Risk scores:

- Unable to persuade or influence others

- Whimsical, impractical, and eccentric

- Creative, but sometimes too extreme

- Preoccupied with their own ideas

- Unconventional and nonconforming

- Unaware of how they impact others

Performance Implications of High Risk Scores (90%–100%)

People with High Risk scores seem playful, innovative, and unconventional. They tend to think and act in ways that are unusual, different, striking, and at times, even odd. They believe that their opinions matter greatly, and they take pride in being original and different. They may have trouble selling their ideas because they are playful, test limits, and have lapses in judgment that can compromise their credibility. These people change focus quickly and frequently and make surprising decisions. Although they can be insightful and visionary, others may find them challenging to work with because they tend to be eccentric, unpredictable, and preoccupied with their own ideas.

Performance Implications of Moderate Risk Scores (70%–89%)

People with Moderate Risk scores seem clever, imaginative, interesting, and inventive. They tend to be original, curious, and unconventional and have a unique way of interpreting events and expressing their views. Although they may be a resource for vision and innovation, working with them can be hard because they are unpredictable, make impractical decisions, have ideas that seem to come "out of left field," get lost in thought, and ignore feedback.

Performance Implications of Low Risk Scores (40%–69%)

Individuals with Low Risk scores seem steady, grounded, and sensible. They seem able to focus on their work, are practically minded, and seldom take extreme positions on issues. Those who score on the higher end of the range may seem distracted by their own ideas and struggle to execute them. Those who score on the lower end of the range tend to be restrained and more conventional in their thinking.

Performance Implications of No Risk Scores (0%–39%)

People with No Risk scores seem quiet, steady, rational, and practical. They are modest, reserved, and have conventional views. They are very good at staying on task, making practical decisions, and not wasting time or showing off. They are unlikely to be sources of innovation and change.

Table 25 contains definitions for Imaginative's subscales.

Table 25: Imaginative Subscales

Subscale	Definition
Eccentric	Expressing unusual views that can be either creative or merely strange; tendency to be absorbed in these ideas
Special Sensitivity	Believing that one has special abilities to see things others do not and understand things others cannot
Creative Thinking	Believing that one is unusually creative, easily bored, and confident in one's imaginative problem-solving ability

Scale 10—Diligent

The Diligent scale concerns behaviors ranging from being relaxed, tolerant, and willing to delegate to being meticulous, picky, and overly critical. Important areas of concern include being obsessive, perfectionistic, and hard to please. Managers with high scores may tend to disempower their subordinates.

The following behaviors are typically associated with Moderate to High Risk scores:

• Perfectionistic

• Controlling

• Micromanaging and reluctant to delegate

• Unable to prioritize tasks

• Stubborn

• Slow to make decisions

Performance Implications of High Risk Scores (90%–100%)

People with High Risk scores seem polite, detail oriented, hardworking, intensely professional, and uncomfortable with ambiguity. They tend to maintain stringent standards of performance for themselves and others and take pride in being conscientious and detail oriented. These people often make every issue a top priority, rarely praise subordinates, and find delegating difficult. They tend to micromanage and be critical, demanding, and stubborn.

Performance Implications of Moderate Risk Scores (70%–89%)

People with Moderate Risk scores are perceived as polite, conscientious, hardworking, and careful about details. They tend to plan and be well organized and perfectionistic. They provide their staff with structure, direction, and feedback but may find letting others make their own mistakes, which is how some people learn, difficult. Although they are good corporate citizens, others may find them hard to work with because they want to do everything themselves, supervise others closely, and can be inflexible and resistant to change.

Performance Implications of Low Risk Scores (40%–69%)

People with Low Risk scores seem flexible, open to suggestions, and tolerant of mistakes. They know how to prioritize, willingly delegate, and provide their staff with learning opportunities. As coaches and mentors, they will be approachable and available but may be somewhat reluctant to give others critical feedback. Those who score on the higher end of the range tend to remain focused on the details and may struggle to delegate tasks. Those who score on the lower end of the range can change directions quickly and tolerate ambiguity but may not seem to care about holding their staff accountable.

Performance Implications of No Risk Scores (0%–39%)

Individuals with No Risk scores seem tolerant, flexible, and relaxed about rules. They prioritize tasks appropriately, routinely delegate tasks, and provide their staff with learning opportunities. However, they may not seem to care about the quality of their staff's performance and fail to hold them accountable, which can lead staff to think they are performing better than they are.

Table 26 contains definitions for Diligent's subscales.

Table 26: Diligent Subscales

Subscale	Definition
Standards	Having exceptionally high standards of performance for oneself and others
Perfectionistic	Perfectionistic about the quality of work products and obsessed with the details of their completion
Organized	Meticulous and inflexible about schedules, timing, rules, and procedures

Scale 11—Dutiful

The Dutiful scale concerns behaviors ranging from being independent and willing to challenge authority to being loyal, compliant, and reluctant to challenge authority. Areas of concern include being overly eager to please bosses and reluctant to act independently. People with high scores may seem pleasant and agreeable but are unwilling to support their subordinates' legitimate complaints about management.

Typical behaviors associated with Moderate to High Risk scores include the following:

• Compliant and conforming

• Reluctant to make independent decisions

• Staunch and unwavering support of the status quo

• Dependable corporate citizens

• Strong desire to please authorities

• Hesitant to advocate for subordinates

Performance Implications of High Risk Scores (90%–100%)

People with High Risk scores seem obliging, predictable, unassuming, and compliant. They are comfortable following rules, work hard to avoid "rocking the boat," and seem eager to please their bosses. They defer to the judgment of higher-ups and are reluctant to challenge the status quo. They may promise their bosses more than they can deliver and may not stick up for their subordinates. Although they are model corporate citizens, others may find working with them challenging because they can be indecisive, reluctant to take initiative, and can rely excessively on others to provide direction.

Performance Implications of Moderate Risk Scores (70%–89%)

People with Moderate Risk scores seem agreeable, pleasant, and cooperative. They support corporate policy, keep others informed, and are eager to please their superiors. They are polite, approachable, and do not like controversy. Although they make positive first impressions, others may find them hard to work with because they seem reluctant to make decisions on their own and seem unduly careful to please their superiors.

Performance Implications of Low Risk Scores (40%–69%)

People with Low Risk scores seem self-starting, independent, and loyal to their staff. They are willing to support, encourage, and develop others. They prefer to work in teams when the activity's purpose is clear and well defined; otherwise, they prefer to set their own agenda. They tend to be willing to take initiative and are able to handle controversy and disagreements with poise. Those who score on the higher end of the range may seek approval from their superiors more frequently than those who score on the lower end of the range.

Performance Implications of No Risk Scores (0%–39%)

Individuals with No Risk scores seem independent, self-reliant, and tough minded. They are willing to challenge people in authority, are not easily discouraged by negative feedback, and will stick up for their subordinates. They can tolerate ambiguity, enjoy challenges, make decisions without prior approval, and will take steps to develop their staff. They could seem rebellious and argumentative.

Table 27 contains definitions for Dutiful's subscales.

Table 27: Dutiful Subscales

Subscale	Definition
Indecisive	Overly reliant on others for advice and reluctant to make decisions or act independently
Ingratiating	Excessively eager to please one's superiors, telling them what they want to hear and never contradicting them
Conforming	Taking pride in supporting one's superiors and following their orders regardless of one's personal opinion

Factor Structure of the HDS

As noted in Chapter 4, the HDS has a three-factor structure. There is a "Moving Away" factor (Excitable, Skeptical, Cautious, Reserved, and Leisurely), a "Moving Against" factor (Bold, Mischievous, Colorful, and Imaginative), and a "Moving Toward" factor (Diligent and Dutiful).

The following describes the three syndromes defined by elevations on all the scales within each factor:

- Moving Away—This syndrome is characterized by florid emotional displays that swing between passionate enthusiasm and intense distaste for people or projects (Excitable). The person is keenly alert for signs of betrayal and/or disapproval, and if they detect these signs, they will challenge, accuse, confront, and retaliate (Skeptical). Beneath the prickly exterior, this person is insecure and afraid of being criticized (Cautious), resentful of superiors (Leisurely), but withdrawn, remote, and preferring to work alone (Reserved). Therefore, the insecurity and resentment may be difficult to detect.

- Moving Against—People typifying this syndrome seem bright, charismatic, and confident to the point of arrogance (Bold); seek excitement and test limits (Mischievous); self-dramatizing, exuberant, and impulsive (Colorful); and creative and innovative to the point of eccentricity (Imaginative). Leaders often display this syndrome because these scales create an aura that others find attractive. The downside is that people with high scores on these scales often manipulate and exploit others, who at some point begin to resent it.

- Moving Toward—This syndrome is defined by obedience, conscientiousness, and a need for control. Managers appreciate such people because they are hardworking and compliant (Diligent). They do what they are asked and avoid taking any actions beyond what their managers have directed (Dutiful). Over time, they come to be seen as unwilling to take initiative or independent action. They may disappoint busy managers who need them to take more initiative as business demands increase. They also disempower their direct reports by micromanaging them.

The three HDS factors can also be defined from strategies that individuals use to influence people:

- Intimidation—"You force me to tell you how much I have become disappointed with you" (Excitable). "I have been taken advantage of, and so I am justified in responding in kind" (Skeptical). "I have no option but to point out that your changes could have disastrous consequences" (Cautious). "You say that I don't listen to you, but if you would say something that interests me, I would listen" (Reserved). "The reason I ignore you is that you always interrupt me at a time when you should be doing your own work" (Leisurely).

- Seduction—"I have a talent for this sort of thing, and so if you follow me, things will go well" (Bold). "This problem is complex from the point of view of the decision-makers, but I have them eating out of my hand" (Mischievous). "Many people find me fascinating, and so if you join me, we can get things moving again" (Colorful). "The reason we are having trouble is because no one can see the possibilities that I do. If you follow my suggestions, we can leave all these problems behind" (Imaginative).

- Control—"You need to give me everything I need because I get things done, they are done right, and they are done ahead of schedule" (Diligent). "I have been loyal to you, letting you make the decisions and following you without question. Now that I need your support, I am sure you won't let me down" (Dutiful).

People with low HDS scores on all these factors seem bland and are unable to significantly influence others.

Chapter 6
Motives, Values, Preferences Inventory

The Motives, Values, Preferences Inventory (MVPI) evaluates people's values, career interests, and unconscious biases. These values, interests, and biases concern what people want and will work to attain or avoid. By assessing values, the inventory ultimately focuses on identity—the "inside" of personality—because values define our identities. Our identities concern the people that we think we are and that others only dimly understand. Some identities are a better fit for some careers than others; making good career decisions depends on understanding the values that form our identities.

The MVPI provides three kinds of information: First, it describes a person's unconscious biases—assumptions about the world that people think are true for everyone but are actually specific to them (e.g., the importance of money). Second, the person's MVPI identifies optimal occupational choices based on their values. Third, the MVPI tells about the kind of culture this person will create for their subordinates if they become managers, because not all cultures are equally valuable.

Origins of the MVPI

The MVPI scales concern universal themes in the literature on motivation. We reviewed 80 years of research on motives, values, and interests and developed 10 content scales. We were influenced by the taxonomies developed by Spranger (1928); Allport (1961); Murray (1938); Allport et al. (1960); and Holland (1966, 1985). Although the labels used for various taxonomies' dimensions differ, there is considerable overlap in the attitudes, values, needs, interests, goals, and commitments that they regard as important. Gregory (1992) summarizes these motivational constructs (see Table 28), indicating how their content aligns with the 10 MVPI scales. Because the history of these constructs' history is useful for understanding the measurement goals for the MVPI scales, we highlight some views that have influenced our taxonomy of motives.

Recognition Motives

The need to be recognized and paid attention to is an important motive in human affairs; it also differs from the power motive. Spranger (1928); Allport et al. (1960); and Novacek and Lazarus (1990) combine power and recognition, but Murray (1938) distinguishes between power and recognition with his achievement and dominance needs (power) and his exhibition needs (recognition). Gregory (1992) proposes that the need for recognition may apply to all of Holland's types because the theme tends to resemble a trait more than a type.

Power Motives

Spranger's (1928) political attitude includes achievement, aggression, status, and dominance, all part of the power motive. Allport et al. (1960) describe the political man as primarily focusing on achieving power. Murray's needs for achievement and

Table 28: Logical Taxonomy of Motives, Attitudes, Values, Needs, Interests, Goals, and Commitments

MVPI	Attitudes: Spranger	Values: Allport, Vernon, & Lindzey	Needs: Murray	Interests: Holland	Goals: Richards	Goals: Wicker, Lambert, Richardson, & Kahler	Goals: Pervin	Commitments: Novacek & Lazarus
Recognition	Political	Political	Exhibition		Prestige	Competitive, Ambition	Aggression-Power	Power/Achievement
Power	Political	Political	Achievement, Dominance	Enterprising	Prestige	Competitive, Ambition	Aggression-Power	Power/Achievement
Hedonism	Aesthetic		Sex, Play		Hedonistic		Relaxation-Fun-Friendship	Sensation Seeking
Altruistic	Social	Social	Nurturance	Social	Altruistic	Interpersonal Concern	Affection-Support	Altruism
Affiliation	Social	Social	Affiliation	Social			Relaxation-Fun-Friendship	Sensation Seeking
Tradition	Religious	Religious			Religious			Personal Growth
Security			Succorance, Infavoidance	Conventional			Reduce Tension-Conflict-Threat	Stress Avoidance
Commerce	Economic	Economic	Acquisition	Conventional				Power/Achievement
Aesthetics	Aesthetic	Aesthetic	Sentience	Artistic	Artistic			
Science	Theoretical	Theoretical	Understanding	Investigative	Scientific			Sensation Seeking

Source: Gregory, 1992. Reprinted with permission.

dominance closely fit with the power motive. The power motive is clearly aligned with Holland's enterprising type. Holland's enterprising type seeks leadership positions, values autonomy, and always wants to be in charge. Holland describes enterprising types as seeking power and being dominant, enthusiastic, and energetic.

Hedonistic Motives

None of Spranger's (1928) attitudes resemble hedonistic motives. Murray's (1938) needs for sex and play contain elements that resemble hedonism; erotic pleasure is the basis of the need for sex, and having fun is the basis of the need for play. Holland has no type analogous to the hedonistic motive. Novacek and Lazarus (1990) identify a sensation-seeking dimension that emphasizes sexual pleasure, fun, free time, and excitement.

Altruistic Motives

Altruistic motives resemble affiliation motives; Spranger's (1928) social attitude and Holland's social type capture part of this construct. However, the distinction between affiliation and altruism is nicely reflected in Murray's (1938) need for nurturance. Nurturance focuses on helping, protecting, caring for, and curing those in need, while affiliation concerns wanting friendship and needing to be around others. Novacek and Lazarus (1990) identify a dimension called altruism, which they describe as the desire to help and support others, as well as being willing to make sacrifices for them.

Affiliation Motives

Spranger's (1928) social attitude highlights the desire for interaction and positive interpersonal relations. Murray's (1938) need for affiliation is one of the best-known motives in his taxonomy; it emphasizes a desire for friendship. Holland's social type wants to be helpful, identifies with charitable activities, and seeks out opportunities for social interaction.

Tradition Motives

The tradition motives resemble Spranger's (1928) religious attitudes, which are concerned with moral issues and conservative values. Novacek and Lazarus (1990) describe a personal growth dimension that contains the moral, ethical, and spiritual themes associated with the tradition motives, particularly in the desire to be fair and just, and the need to develop a philosophy of life. None of Holland's types endorse the tradition motives.

Security Motives

As seen in Table 28, the security motives are not well mapped by the major motivational theorists. Because the construct concerns a need for certainty, control, and order, it resembles Murray's (1938) definition of the needs for succorance and infavoidance. The succorance need focuses on the desire to be protected and cared for, whereas the infavoidance need involves the desire to avoid blame and social censure. There is some overlap between the security motives and Holland's description of conventional types as being conforming, conservative, and methodical.

Commerce Motives

Interest in business and making money are the core of commercial motives, and this dimension can be traced back to Spranger's (1928) economic attitude, which emphasized the desire to control resources and acquire material possessions. Allport et al.'s (1960) economic man is interested in business and the accumulation of wealth. Holland's conventional type is interested in business, identifies with successful businesspeople, and wants to work in finance and commerce. These types are described as conservative, conforming, unimaginative, and methodical.

Aesthetic Motives

Spranger (1928) defined the aesthete as a person who enjoys the pleasures of the body and the arts. Murray's (1938) need for sentience, which he described as seeking out sensuous feelings and impressions, is similar to Spranger's (1928) aesthetic attitude. Holland's (1987) artistic type values the world of beauty, identifies with artists of various disciplines, and aspires to work in creative pursuits.

Holland describes artistic types as creative, sensitive, imaginative, and nonconforming.

Science Motives

Spranger's (1928) theoretical attitude emphasizes a need to name, classify, and logically analyze nature. Similarly, Allport et al. (1960) proposed that the theoretical man seeks to discover truth through empirical, critical, and logical means. Holland's investigative type values logic, analysis, and the pursuit of knowledge. The investigative type enjoys science and identifies with scientists. Holland describes the investigative type as intellectual, scholarly, analytical, and curious.

Initial Development

The MVPI contains 150 statements to which respondents indicate "agree strongly," "agree," "disagree," or "disagree strongly." Each scale contains 15 items derived rationally from hypotheses about the likes, dislikes, and assumptions of an "ideal" exemplar of each motive. The scales are composed of three themes: (a) Drivers, which concern a person's enthusiasms and passions; (b) Occupations, which concern a person's preferred work activities and settings; and (c) Unconscious Biases, which concern passionately held beliefs that a person thinks everyone shares.

There are no correct or incorrect responses for the MVPI items; therefore, there is no need for validity or faking keys. Among the 10 scales, no items overlap. The items were screened for content that might seem offensive or an invasion of privacy. There are no items concerning sexual preferences, religious beliefs, criminal or illegal behavior, racial/ethnic attitudes, or attitudes about disabled individuals. There are no items that could be used to determine physical or mental disabilities; the MVPI is not a medical examination.

General Interpretive Guidelines for the MVPI

- The MVPI provides three kinds of feedback. First, it reveals a person's unconscious biases—that is, their assumptions about how much other people agree with them regarding important social and political attitudes. Second, the MVPI provides suggestions regarding a person's potential occupational choices. Third, the MVPI indicates the kind of culture a person will create when in leadership positions. In addition, group MVPI results can help teams better understand their areas of potential conflict; it can also help organizations understand their unique cultures.

- The MVPI can be used in a wide variety of employee selection and development situations.

- The relative degree of person–job fit can be determined by comparing a person's higher scores on the MVPI with the prevailing values of an organization.

- Scores above the 65th percentile are considered high. These are the true drivers that actively shape people's lives. Managers should pay close attention to these scores when dealing with employees.

- Scores between the 36th and 64th percentiles are considered average. These are important value considerations for career planning.

- Scores below the 35th percentile are considered to be low. These concern the themes that people dislike and seek to avoid.

- If a profile has no high scores, then the average scores are considered to be drivers.

- The MVPI profiles of leaders predict the working environments that they will create for their employees.

- The MVPI profile of the top leadership will be a key driver of organizational culture.

- The interpretive statements for each scale are empirically based.

MVPI Global Portability

The MVPI has been used for more than 40 years, during which time it has proven to be a valuable tool for understanding individual motivation and career drivers. Perhaps even more important from an international perspective is understanding the types of environments leaders create. We have engaged in large-scale translation efforts over the years. The MVPI is currently available online in the following languages:

- Arabic
- Azerbaijani
- Bulgarian
- Chinese (Simplified)
- Chinese (Traditional)
- Croatian
- Czech
- Danish
- Dutch
- English (Australian and New Zealand)
- English (Greek)
- English (Indian)
- English (Kenyan)
- English (Middle Eastern)
- English (South African)
- English (UK)
- English (US)
- Estonian
- Finnish
- French (Canadian)
- French (Parisian)
- German
- Greek
- Hebrew
- Hungarian
- Icelandic
- Indonesian
- Italian
- Japanese
- Korean
- Latvian
- Macedonian
- Malaysian
- Montenegrin
- Norwegian
- Polish
- Portuguese (Brazilian)
- Portuguese (European)
- Romanian
- Russian

- Serbian
- Slovak
- Slovenian
- Spanish (Castilian)
- Spanish (Latin American)

- Swedish
- Thai
- Turkish
- Ukrainian
- Vietnamese

We have developed an international research archive for the MVPI, which includes normative data and validation research. The results support the MVPI's global portability.

Chapter 7
How to Interpret the Motives, Values, Preferences Inventory

Recognition

The Recognition scale concerns individual differences in the desire to be visible in one's social network, profession, and larger community. People with low scores seem modest and unassuming; people with high scores want to be seen, recognized, and honored. Possible careers for people with high scores include work in the entertainment industry, the performing arts, acting, politics, public speaking of any kind, and sales.

Performance Implications of Low Scores (0%–35%)

People with low Recognition scores seem shy, modest, and reclusive—perhaps to a fault (check for a high Reserved score). They do not expect or enjoy praise and attention, they avoid being the center of attention, and they think other people also want to avoid calling attention to themselves. They prefer to work behind the scenes. Regardless of their actual performance, these people may tend to be underpaid and underappreciated, and their professional advancement can be limited. As managers, they will create a "heads down, just do your job" culture that may frustrate team members with higher Recognition needs.

Performance Implications of Average Scores (36%–64%)

People with average Recognition scores tend to prefer environments where they have opportunities to be with others and will be recognized for their achievements. These people may share credit with others, but they speak up when they are due some credit for important accomplishments. As managers, they acknowledge the performance of team members but may miss opportunities to promote their team's successes as a whole.

Tips to consider:

- Those who score on the higher end of average scores seem to enjoy the spotlight and will work to gain it. As managers, they will try to recognize their team's performance.

- Those who score on the lower end of average scores seem somewhat modest, retiring, and easily embarrassed when attention is on them. As managers, they may assume that their team has minimal needs to have their work acknowledged publicly.

Performance Implications of High Scores (65%–100%)

People with high Recognition scores enjoy being on stage and the center of attention, with all eyes fixed on them, and they plan to make it happen. They are rarely embarrassed, dislike being ignored, want visibility and approval, and assume others want it too. They seek high-profile work assignments and make the most of such assignments. As a result, when others are trying to work, they may find these people disruptive. As managers, they try to acknowledge the performance of their team but often as a reflection of their own performance.

Recognition and Leadership

Leaders with high Recognition scores want others to appreciate them. They expect to be admired and may be annoyed when they are not. On one hand, this puts pressure on their staff to be appropriately admiring. On the other hand, high Recognition leaders can impose recognition on their subordinates, which can create unexpected tensions. Low Recognition leaders can create a staff that feels unappreciated.

Recognition and Culture

A high Recognition culture is one that acknowledges accomplishment, productivity, and apparent success in public fashion. In addition, the organization will self-consciously strive to ensure that clients and competitors understand the significance of its performance. This is a culture with the leader as the star. People who want to be left alone to do their work tend not to fit in well in this environment.

Unexpected Interpretation

People with high Recognition scores are not passive attention-seekers; on the contrary, they tend to think other people find them fascinating and, consequently, are always ready to show others just how true that is.

Power

The Power scale concerns wanting to succeed, get results, contribute to one's organization or profession, and create a legacy for oneself. People with low scores are cooperative, accommodating, and indifferent to success; people with high scores are competitive, energetic, and achievement oriented, and have plans for their careers. Possible careers for people with high scores for Power include any work that provides opportunities for rapid performance-based promotions, opportunities to make a difference, and opportunities to enjoy success based on hard work and accomplishment.

Performance Implications of Low Scores (0%–35%)

People with low scores on Power appear quiet, passive, flexible, and compliant. They may not seem to have a strong sense of urgency, and they dislike being pushed to get things done. Work is something they do to be able to pursue their real interests. Usually not very strategic about their careers, they are reluctant to lead. As managers, they tend to leave people alone and rarely hold them accountable.

Performance Implications of Average Scores (36%–64%)

People with average scores on Power likely want to be successful and take pride in their achievements but also realize that there is more to life than a job. As managers, they cooperate with other managers, share credit with their teams, and keep their team's morale stable under pressure.

Tips to consider:

- Those who score on the higher end of average scores seem more active, energetic, and willing to take initiative. As managers, they actively monitor their team's progress and encourage team achievement.

- Those who score on the lower end of average scores may lack a clear career and focus. At work they tend to accept directions and do what is required. As managers, they tend to be hands-off and less results driven.

Performance Implications of High Scores (65%–100%)

People with high scores on Power seem intense, passionate, and in a hurry to get things done. They dislike delays, inefficiencies, and low-performing team members. They want to win and dislike the appearance of losing. They seek responsibility and will take the initiative to achieve results. They do not understand people who do not focus on their career and lack a sense of urgency. They may appear domineering, overly competitive, or intimidating to their teams. As managers, they will be results oriented and keep their team accountable to deliver the planned work.

Power and Leadership

Leaders with high scores for Power are achievement oriented and want to make a difference while creating a legacy. They value productivity and have little tolerance for direct reports with mediocre performance. They tend to push others for results and make sure projects get done on time. At the same time, however, they may tend to exercise too much top-down control, may not be good team players, and may compete with the members of their own teams. Leaders with low scores for Power tend not to push for results or hold people accountable for their performance.

Power and Culture

A culture characterized by high Power is aggressive, competitive, and results oriented. It tracks its performance vis-à-vis the competition; sets ambitious goals; minimizes wasted motion, meetings, and pointless discussions; and evaluates itself in terms of what it can accomplish. The "heroes" of the organization will be those who make substantive, measurable contributions. The outcasts will be "the lazy" and/or ineffectual.

Unexpected Interpretation

People with high scores for Power are strategic about their careers; consequently, they are always alert for new opportunities to advance their agendas, even when they seem to be relaxing.

Hedonism

The Hedonism scale concerns wanting to have fun, enjoy oneself, and entertain others. Everyone likes to have fun, but people with high Hedonism scores often seem to make a career of it. People with low Hedonism scores seem restrained and austere; people with high scores seem spontaneous and festive and to seek fun. Possible careers for people with high scores include food services, catering, and hospitality; vacation and travel planning; wedding and event planning; and tour guiding.

Performance Implications of Low Scores (0%–35%)

People with low scores on Hedonism appear formal, restrained, disciplined, and proper. They seem serious, self-controlled, and focused on their work. They do not like to waste time and can be impatient with others who seem to engage in frivolous and/ or nonproductive behavior. As managers, they create highly disciplined teams but may cause burnout in the more socially driven team members.

Performance Implications of Average Scores (36%–64%)

People with average scores on Hedonism prefer a flexible work environment that allows them to set their own priorities. As managers, these people tend to strike a balance between work and play. They encourage breaks and fun activities but not at the expense of undermining deadlines and quality work.

Tips to consider:

- Those who score on the higher end of average scores seem more casual, relaxed, companionable, and concerned about others' enjoyment. As managers, they tend to be easygoing and create an informal and spontaneous atmosphere.

- Those who score on the lower end of average scores seem serious, controlled, and well behaved. They do not like wasting resources on nonessential activities. As managers, they tend to create a highly focused and austere atmosphere and may dislike frivolous team members.

Performance Implications of High Scores (65%–100%)

People with high scores on Hedonism seem informal, self-indulgent, and fun loving. They enjoy organizing and attending social events and entertaining others, even though they usually have a business agenda in mind during the events (check for a high Power score). They are active, energetic, and inclusive, thinking that everyone should be able to combine business with pleasure, relax, and have a good time. As managers, they create a casual, relaxed, "work hard, play hard" culture.

Hedonism and Leadership

Leaders with high scores for Hedonism are motivated by opportunities to relax and have fun, and they enjoy entertaining others. However, they often have an agenda behind their jolly façade. They tend to create an informal culture characterized by office parties, celebration of staff accomplishments, and an overall sense of fun. However, not everyone has a sense of humor, and some staff may think these leaders lack seriousness. Leaders with low scores for Hedonism are all business all the time.

Hedonism and Culture

A high Hedonism culture is characterized by an ethos of "work hard/play hard"; people strive to perform at a high level and then take time to relax, celebrate, and have fun. There is a clear awareness that having fun is as much a part of the culture as effortful striving, and there may even be a "party budget." The "heroes" of the organization will be those who are the most entertaining. The outcasts will be "party poopers."

Unexpected Interpretation

People with high Hedonism scores may seem like agenda-free party animals, but in fact, they are watchful, alert, socially insightful, and use social occasions to gather information about competitors and career opportunities.

Altruistic

The Altruistic scale concerns wanting to help people who need assistance, including the young and inexperienced and those who are less fortunate. People with low scores seem task oriented, tough, and independent, strongly believing in the importance of self-reliance. People with high scores value fairness and equality and seem sympathetic, compassionate, and concerned about the welfare of the less fortunate. Possible careers for people with high scores include teaching, health care, social work, counseling, human resources, animal welfare, and philanthropic activities.

Performance Implications of Low Scores (0%–35%)

People with low scores on Altruistic seem tough, matter-of-fact, demanding, and indifferent to issues of injustice and inequality. They believe in the importance of individual effort, independence, personal accountability, and self-reliance. These people seem indifferent to others' emotions, preferring to work in task- instead of people-focused environments. As managers, they may insist that team members be more self-reliant and may be stricter about performance appraisals.

Performance Implications of Average Scores (36%–64%)

People with average scores on Altruistic can balance compassion with concern for the bottom line. They enjoy helping others and are more likely to contribute money over personal time to help others. As managers, these people can be friendly and compassionate but prefer to enable and empower team members to resolve problems on their own.

Tips to consider:

- Those who score on the higher end of average scores seem sympathetic to problems of inequality and injustice and willing to help others when asked. As managers, they will tend to do more coaching for success and encourage teamwork.

- Those who score on the lower end of average scores tend to favor self-reliance, independence, and personal accountability. As managers, they tend to focus on performance management and keeping team members accountable.

Performance Implications of High Scores (65%–100%)

People with high scores on Altruistic are sensitive to the needs of others and look for opportunities to assist the disadvantaged. They care about societal well-being, animal welfare, and the environment; seem sympathetic and empathic; and enjoy helping others. As managers, they tend to be very good coaches and mentors, foster teamwork, and seem willing to give problem employees a second chance.

Altruism and Leadership

Leaders with high scores for Altruism enjoy teaching and encouraging others. They tend to create a culture marked by fairness, civility, respect, and an emphasis on personal growth and development. Some people may think Altruistic leaders do not care about accountability and results. Leaders with low Altruism scores will emphasize self-reliance and provide their staff with little coaching or encouragement.

Altruism and Culture

Altruistic cultures care about the morale and well-being of the staff; they encourage people to develop their talents and fulfill their potential while providing them with the resources to do so. Interactions at work are characterized by respect, consideration, and mutual support. Such organizations tend also to be involved in the larger social community. The "heroes" of the organization will be those who are the most supportive and selfless, and selfish people will be a bad fit for the organization.

Unexpected Interpretation

People with high Altruism scores often champion unpopular causes—for example, civil rights, environmental preservation—which makes them seem eccentric and rebellious, but beneath the surface, they are typically conventional and peaceful.

Affiliation

The Affiliation scale concerns enjoying social interaction, wanting to join and/or build social networks and participate in group or team efforts. People with low scores seem shy, independent, and withdrawn. People with high scores search for opportunities to interact, meet new people, share gossip, and find social acceptance and affirmation. Possible careers for people with high scores for Affiliation include consulting, sales and marketing, politics, advertising, and public relations.

Performance Implications of Low Scores (0%–35%)

People with low scores on Affiliation seem shy, independent, withdrawn, and possibly aloof (check for a low Reserved score). They are not interested in networking, developing new relationships, or staying up to date with the insider gossip. They prefer to be left alone to do their work and dislike meetings and working as part of a team. These people assume that others also want to be left alone. Their natural reticence creates a risk that their contributions may be overlooked. As managers, they tend to be remote and uncommunicative, often leaving their staff to figure things out for themselves.

Performance Implications of Average Scores (36%–64%)

People with average scores on Affiliation tend to communicate openly and provide information and feedback to their teams. As managers, they tend to enjoy both quiet, task-focused time and collaboration with their team but may not deepen the relationships with the team members to achieve loyalty and retention.

Tips to consider:

- Those who score on the higher end of average scores purposefully reach out to and stay in contact with others. As managers, they tend to communicate with and engage their teams.

- Those who score on the lower end of average scores seem to prefer more privacy and individual work. As managers, they tend to communicate infrequently and provide only limited guidance to their teams.

Performance Implications of High Scores (65%–100%)

People with high scores on Affiliation need a rich, full, and active social life and tend vigorously to pursue it. They enjoy building social networks, cultivating new friends, reaching out to others, and staying informed about changes in people's status. These people enjoy meetings and working as part of teams. They assume others need as much social contact as they do; as a result, their coworkers may sometimes find them disruptive. As managers, they appear very approachable, communicate frequently with their teams, and prioritize team cohesion and morale over productivity.

Affiliation and Leadership

Leaders who have high scores for Affiliation love social interaction. Consequently, they tend to create cultures characterized by frequent communication among and between units; there will likely be many meetings and spontaneous special-purpose work teams. Leaders with low scores for Affiliation tend to be remote and task oriented and communicate infrequently.

Affiliation and Culture

High Affiliation cultures feature a strong tendency toward social interaction. The official and unofficial practices and procedures tend to maximize social contact. This includes frequent scheduled and unscheduled meetings, regular communication within and between units, and organizing the office space to encourage interaction. The "heroes" of the organization will be those who are most popular; the outcasts will be the loners.

Unexpected Interpretation

High scorers seem charming, sociable, talkative, and approachable, but beneath their surface affability, they are often quite ambitious and agenda driven, and their interactions with people are often intelligence-gathering operations.

Tradition

The Tradition scale concerns individual differences in respect for hierarchy, history, established procedures, and legitimate authority. People with high scores seem conventional and defend the customs and beliefs of their family, tribe, culture, nation, or ethnic heritage, which are important sources of their personal identity. People with low scores seem open minded, unconventional, irreverent, and value change and experimentation for their own sake; they see tradition as "the dead hand of the past," as something to be overcome. Potential careers for high scorers include military service, law enforcement, environmental preservation, archeology, historical research, and joining a religious order.

Performance Implications of Low Scores (0%–35%)

People with low scores on Tradition seem unorthodox, unconventional, innovative, and disruptive. They value change—both as a means of progress and as an end in itself—and rarely support the status quo. They greatly dislike complacency and self-satisfaction, which means they play an important role in any organization. They also assume that other people are as comfortable with change and restructuring as they are, which is often not the case. As managers, they appeal to team members who value innovation but sometimes may create confusion and neglect important rules and protocols.

Performance Implications of Average Scores (36%–64%)

People with average scores on Tradition are comfortable with ritual, routine, fixed schedules, and standard operating procedures. They respect tradition and history as guides to behavior but are also open to doing things in new ways. As managers, they are good at implementing incremental changes but may struggle when innovative decisions need to be made.

Tips to consider:

- Those who score on the higher end of average scores appreciate reporting hierarchies and encourage others to do so as well. As managers, they tend to uphold established systems and procedures but may be impatient with those who challenge them unnecessarily.

- Those who score on the lower end of average scores see change as inherently good. As managers, they energize their teams for change but may be too impulsive and unpredictable to control the execution of change.

Performance Implications of High Scores (65%–100%)

People with high scores on Tradition understand that, to function properly, organizations need rules, structure, and hierarchy. They respect authority and chains of command, supporting efforts to maintain them. They value concepts such as tradition, honor, duty, and service, and they proudly support them. Slow to adopt necessary changes, they do not understand people who think the system needs to be restructured. As managers, they are seen as reliable and predictable but may be too rigid to consider alternative, less established viewpoints and work practices of their team members.

Tradition and Leadership

Leaders with high scores on Tradition tend to emphasize rules, procedures, and customs that characterized their organization in its glory days; they will be leaders from the "old school" who pursue success by doing things "the right way," and they are likely to resist fads and innovation. Leaders with low Tradition scores tend to be innovative, tolerant of nonconformance, and like experimenting with new methods or procedures; conversely, they may seek change without considering the benefits of historical precedence.

Tradition and Culture

High Tradition cultures feature a strong tendency toward rewarding adherence to classic forms and behavioral patterns. They tend to have official dress codes and teach newcomers the principles of their founders. Pride is taken in doing things the way they have always been done. The "heroes" of the organization will be those who are most zealous in keeping the traditions; the outcasts will be the innovators.

Unexpected Interpretation

People with high Tradition scores often appear resistant to innovation and stifle organizational changes. However, many of their practices have been tested and proven over time, and if properly engaged and have conviction, they can contribute considerably to efficient, controlled change.

Security

The Security scale concerns valuing structure, predictability, and control and efforts to minimize chance, insecurity, and risk. People with high scores plan carefully to control financial exposure, employment uncertainty, environmental change, and criticism. Low scorers enjoy exploring the unknown, testing limits, innovating, and having the freedom to fail. Potential careers for high scorers include accounting, corporate law, cybersecurity, actuarial work, and insurance adjustment.

Performance Implications of Low Scores (0%–35%)

People with low Security scores seem impatient, curious, imaginative, adventurous, and reward-seeking. They enjoy taking risks and testing limits, are comfortable with ambiguity and uncertainty, and like feedback on their performance. They are unconcerned about job security and prefer fast-paced environments where risk-taking and experimentation are rewarded. As managers, they can serve as change agents in risk-averse organizations, motivating their teams to embrace experimentation and learn more quickly.

Performance Implications of Average Scores (36%–64%)

People with average Security scores perform well in situations in which the chances of success are certain or the future of the organization is secure. As managers, they can be good change agents if they are guided from above.

Tips to consider:

- Those who score on the higher end of average scores prefer stable, structured, and predictable work environments. As managers, they may be seen as risk avoidant and miss high-stakes opportunities in volatile environments.

- Those who score on the lower end of average scores tend to be more experimental, willing to try new things, and less concerned with job security. As managers, they can motivate their teams to embrace change but need to reassure and guide the team too.

Performance Implications of High Scores (65%–100%)

People with high Security scores seem deliberate, disciplined, risk-averse, and careful. They try to avoid unnecessary risks, financial uncertainty, and easy-to-make mistakes. Others may describe them as polite, detail oriented, and easy to supervise. These people's careers tend to move slowly because they are unwilling to take career risks. As managers, they maintain smooth operations, tight compliance, and a workforce that feels safe to do its best work within a clear, stable framework.

Security and Leadership

Leaders with high Security scores dislike risk and value structure and predictability. They tend to make decisions characterized by caution, explicit fallback options, and fail-safe strategies. Leaders with low Security scores are unafraid of risk, will take chances to advance the business, and will recover from failure and reversals.

Security and Culture

High Security cultures are characterized by a concern about errors, mistakes, and leaks and building processes to guard against undesired eventualities, both real and imagined. These will include security procedures, access codes, oversight plans to guarantee compliance with authorized methods, and an ongoing emphasis on minimizing risk. The "heroes" of the organization will be those who make the fewest mistakes and excel in calling others out; the outcasts will be the experimenters.

Unexpected Interpretation

People with high Security scores are traditionally masculine—which turns out to be associated with tactical, slow, and cautious decision-making; people with low Security scores (who do not seem traditionally masculine) turn out to be the ones who are bold, strategic, and innovative risk-takers.

Commerce

The Commerce scale concerns valuing wealth and financial gain, an interest in realizing profits and finding investment opportunities, and a lifestyle organized around financial planning and profit-making. High scorers are concerned about making money; they are interested in budget and compensation issues and value investment opportunities, financial forecasting, and cost–benefit analyses. Low scorers are unconcerned with wealth and/or financial success and will not spend time, energy, or attention on finance-related issues. Potential careers for people with high scores include sales, banking, finance, investing, and securities trading—all forms of money management.

Performance Implications of Low Scores (0%–35%)

People with low Commerce scores seem more interested in having fun and avoiding conflict than in money or financial success. Having few well-formed career plans, they tend to be easygoing, relaxed, and a bit naïve. They may be pleasant and well-liked, but they rarely push people for results. They are indifferent to commercial values, unconcerned about material success, and lack interest in finance-related issues. As managers, these people think about the company's mission and invest in their team's psychological safety and well-being.

Performance Implications of Average Scores (36%–64%)

People with average Commerce scores believe that money is not a major motivator in their personal or work life. As managers, they keep their budget under control and their teams motivated but may be slow and not aggressive enough in competitive industries.

Tips to consider:

- Those who score on the higher end of average scores are more motivated by financial issues and tend to evaluate themselves in terms of monetary success. As managers, they may put tangible business outcomes above their team's needs.

- Those who score on the lower end of average scores are hesitant about taking on challenges and ambitious projects. As managers, they are less concerned about material success and may not push their team members enough to beat the competition.

Performance Implications of High Scores (65%–100%)

People with high Commerce scores are ambitious, confident, practical, and financially savvy. They are serious about their work, attentive to detail, businesslike, direct, and care deeply about income and material success as forms of self-evaluation. They are most happy in work environments with opportunities to make money and get ahead.

As managers, these people are good at budget stewardship, allocating resources to pragmatic ideas and projects, and mentoring employees toward a good financial mindset.

Commerce and Leadership

Leaders with high Commerce scores are motivated by the bottom line and expect that others will share their enthusiasm for hard work, competition, and the search for commercial success. They will push people for results, and others may think they tend to emphasize profits over people and finances over feelings. Leaders with low scores will seem indifferent to budgets, profitability, deadlines, and other financial issues.

Commerce and Culture

High Commerce cultures emphasize profitability, financial growth, and cost containment. The "heroes" of the culture will be "rainmakers," or the people driving profits, developing the business, or finding effective methods for reducing costs. There will be a constant focus on the "bottom line," sometimes over the short run and possibly at the expense of the long term. The outcasts of the organization will be wastrels and spendthrifts.

Unexpected Interpretation

The stereotype of a high Commerce person is that of a Wall Street Banker: selfish and greedy. However, people with high Commerce scores also have many attractive attributes, including drive, courage, brains, and shrewd political skills.

Aesthetics

The Aesthetics scale concerns individual differences in the preference for form (how things look) versus function (how things work). Low scorers value practicality and functionality, and they are more concerned with how work products perform than how they look. High scorers value innovation, creative problem-solving, and good design and are happiest working in environments that allow experimentation, exploration, and creative self-expression. Possible careers for high scorers include architecture, industrial and interior design, advertising and marketing, commercial art, and website design.

Performance Implications of Low Scores (0%–35%)

People with low Aesthetics scores seem practical, steady, and comfortable with structure. Indifferent to aesthetic considerations, they tend to be conventional, realistic, and efficient. They can persist with boring tasks and are practical problem-solvers. They tend to be unconcerned with artistic or creative initiatives and may resist innovation. Their intense practicality can alienate colleagues who value innovation or visually appealing products. As managers, these people tend to value team members who prioritize functionality and may unintentionally undervalue creative team members.

Performance Implications of Average Scores (36%–64%)

People with average Aesthetics scores combine creativity and practicality and are more concerned with the content rather than the appearance of work products. As managers, they do not allow debates about how to design things perfectly to stall execution but may miss opportunities to use creative appearance as a strategic advantage.

Tips to consider:

- Those who score on the higher end of average scores are happiest working in informal environments, encouraging creativity. As managers, these people will look for creative input from the team but keep project milestones in view.

- Those who score on the lower end of average scores work well in structured, predictable environments and may be less likely to be comfortable with frequent changes in products. As managers, these people may outsource design tasks to those who are more artistically inclined.

Performance Implications of High Scores (65%–100%)

People with high Aesthetics scores seem curious, open minded, rebellious, and impulsive. They are happiest in work environments that allow experimentation, exploration, and creative problem-solving. They enjoy innovation and care about appearance and design issues, as well as the environment in which they work. Their enthusiasm for new, original, and different things can make concentrating on old, dull, repetitive things difficult. As managers, these people encourage their teams to experiment and prototype; they motivate through visionary language and vivid examples.

Aesthetics and Leadership

Leaders with high Aesthetics scores are concerned about the appearance and quality of work products. They value high concept and style, paying attention to appearance and layout issues. Others may think they waste money on nonessentials, but for such leaders, appearance trumps cost every time. Leaders with low scores care about functionality, cost control, and efficiencies, not appearances.

Aesthetics and Culture

A high Aesthetics culture will be characterized by attention to style, appearance, and "good taste." The furniture, wall coverings, rugs, and restrooms will be high quality, often the result of advice from external consultants. Stationery, logos, and reception areas (all aspects of the public face of the organization) will send a message to clients and staff regarding style standards. The heroes of the organization will be those with good taste; the unrefined will be the outcasts.

Unexpected Interpretation

People with high Aesthetics scores may have diva-like characteristics—dramatic, stubborn, and temperamental—and may frustrate others, but the success of many organizations (e.g., Apple) will depend on Aesthetic qualities—that is, the design and marketing of their products.

Science

The Science scale concerns being interested in technology, research, and understanding how things work. Trusting experts' opinions, low scorers prefer to learn from stories rather than data, and they make quick decisions based on experience and intuition; once they have made decisions, they rarely revisit them. High scorers value rationality and data-based decision-making, distrust authority, and believe in checking their work. They prefer to make decisions slowly and then revisit them. Possible careers for high scorers include science and research, engineering, data analytics, product design, and medicine.

Performance Implications of Low Scores (0%–35%)

People with low Science scores seem practical and action oriented and have little patience for abstract analysis. They like to learn by imitating or watching, not by reading and processing data; they solve problems based on experience and intuition. These people are open to all sources of information and are less concerned whether the sources have empirical support or are scientifically accepted. They prefer quick solutions even when problems are complex. As managers, these people make quick decisions in crises but might be biased toward their own solutions.

Performance Implications of Average Scores (36%–64%)

People with average Science scores strike a balance between analysis and action while trying to stay up to date on new technical and business information. They are helpful when solving problems but may need to engage others to find the right solution. As managers, these people like to delegate deep analysis to specialists but may lose some credibility in the eyes of highly technical teams.

Tips to consider:

- Those who score on the higher end of average scores stay up to date on new technical and business information and make decisions in a data-based manner. As managers, these people will seek expert input but will ask probing questions before accepting it.

- Those who score on the lower end of average scores like to learn through stories of firsthand experience and prefer to solve problems based on their gut instinct. As managers, these people keep communication simple and reference data as needed but may make decisions too quickly.

Performance Implications of High Scores (65%–100%)

People with high Science scores seem curious, analytical, and comfortable with technology. They enjoy analyzing problems and like to understand how things work, exploring the underlying factors to reveal answers. Tending to stay informed about new technical and business information, they prefer work environments where they can use data to identify trends, solve problems, or create meaning. They may also seem easily bored, impatient, and argumentative, preferring analysis to action. As managers, these people encourage their teams to challenge assumptions and might be condescending to team members who rely on their intuition.

Science and Leadership

Leaders with high Science scores are logical, disciplined, and empirically minded and prefer data-based decisions. They value rationality and accountability and may be slow to react and make decisions. They tend to be impatient with authority and people who cannot keep up with their thinking. Leaders with low scores value intuition, instinct, and experience, preferring good-enough, quick decisions.

Science and Culture

A high Science culture will focus on the logic and defensibility of plans, goals, decisions, and public statements. People need to justify their positions and opinions with logic and data. Any person's views can be challenged and must be defended satisfactorily. Few decisions will be made arbitrarily or idiosyncratically; policies and procedures will typically be based on evidence and rationality. The "heroes" of the organization will be the smart people; the outcasts will be the "airheads" and slow learners.

Unexpected Interpretation

The good news about people with high Science scores is that they run meetings well and are willing to tackle hard problems; the bad news is that they value problem-solving as an end in itself and will persevere past the point where it is functional.

Chapter 8
Configural Interpretation

The preceding chapters concern how to interpret the scales on the three Hogan inventories (the HPI, the HDS, and the MVPI), focusing on the performance implications of each scale. This information is necessary for understanding the inventories, but certain combinations or configurations of scales provide even more interpretive power.

Configural interpretation involves combining certain scales to gain deeper insight into performance. Configural interpretations require some experience reviewing inventory results. The three inventories contain 28 scales, which works out to 756 possible 2-scale combinations and many other 3-, 4-, 5-, or more scale combinations. Reviewing all these combinations is not possible (or useful). However, certain combinations are more common, and recognizing them can dramatically improve one's ability to interpret the inventories.

This chapter provides some insights into configural interpretation. We start with the HPI as a guide for building increasingly complex interpretations. Then we discuss the configurations associated with occupations. We conclude this chapter with a discussion of frequently occurring "syndrome" configurations.

HPI Interpretation

The easiest way to demonstrate configural interpretations is to use a lookup table for the seven HPI scales, taken two at a time. This approach results in 84 dyads, illustrated in two "lookup" tables, seen here as Tables 29 and 30.

Table 29: HPI Low Score Configurations

			Impact of the Combination
Low Adjustment	High	Ambition	Driven to compete and win while worrying about possibly failing and being criticized.
	Low	Ambition	Fears and avoids failure by choosing low-pressure roles with few demands.
	High	Sociability	Needs social interaction but constantly worries about being rejected or criticized, which results in diminished social skills.
	Low	Sociability	Prone to worry and self-doubt, afraid of being criticized, avoiding social gatherings and public appearances.
	High	Inter. Sens.	Will try to avoid conflict, will be upset when conflicts arise, and will blame self when they occur.
	Low	Inter. Sens.	Will be blunt and confrontational during interactions, then will feel guilty about damaging relationships.

Table 29: (continued): HPI Low Score Configurations

			Impact of the Combination
	High	Prudence	Will follow rules, pay attention to details, work very hard, and feel guilty about breaking almost any rules.
	Low	Prudence	May have issues with anger management and self-control, and may engage in self-defeating defiance of authority.
	High	Inquisitive	Bursts of creative activity will be interrupted by bouts of self-doubt and self-examination.
	Low	Inquisitive	Will resist change or new ideas because the unknown creates anxiety.
	High	Learn. App.	Will be driven to stay up to date to avoid feeling anxious about not being "in the know" about new developments.
	Low	Learn. App.	Seeks learning opportunities that are immediately actionable but may not proactively stay up to date without feedback to do so.
Low Ambition	High	Sociability	Will be lively and outgoing but with few career goals and little focus on achievement.
	Low	Sociability	A follower who allows others to lead and happily goes along as a team player.
	High	Inter. Sens.	Will be pleasant and agreeable but seem meek, noncompetitive, and unwilling to challenge others.
	Low	Inter. Sens.	Will tend to be argumentative or disagreeable but with little desire to "win" such interactions or even make a point.
	High	Prudence	Will follow rules and procedures to get work done but will rarely take initiative even when things go wrong.
	Low	Prudence	Will take shortcuts and do things the easiest possible way, with minimum standards of performance.
	High	Inquisitive	Curious about new ideas and techniques but rarely does anything or commits to a course of action.
	Low	Inquisitive	Will seem passive, even lazy, and will avoid changes or innovations that might create additional work.

Table 29: (continued): HPI Low Score Configurations

			Impact of the Combination
	High	Learn. App.	Will seem smart and well informed but unwilling to take initiative to use new knowledge at work.
	Low	Learn. App.	Will resist training to improve performance or applying new knowledge to improve processes.
Low Sociability	High	Inter. Sens.	Will seldom start new relationships but will be good at maintaining existing relationships.
	Low	Inter. Sens.	Seems quiet and even shy but nonetheless is rather tough and willing to confront others when necessary.
	High	Prudence	Will be task oriented, planful, organized, hardworking, and prefers to work alone.
	Low	Prudence	Will be careless, impulsive, and defiant but usually in a low-profile manner.
	High	Inquisitive	Will be quiet and reserved but curious about what is going on; should be a good listener.
	Low	Inquisitive	Little interest in interacting with others, and no interest in change or innovation.
	High	Learn. App.	Interested in training and knowledge acquisition but doing so while alone.
	Low	Learn. App.	Prefers to learn in an experiential, hands-on fashion without being evaluated.
Low Interpersonal Sensitivity	High	Prudence	Will be blunt and direct and tend to confront people who do not follow rules or pay attention to detail.
	Low	Prudence	Will be impulsive, self-absorbed, confrontational, and a poor team player who ignores feedback.
	High	Inquisitive	Will be curious and open minded, and willing to challenge others' views openly.
	Low	Inquisitive	Should be a tough-minded pragmatist with little tolerance for woolly minded abstractions or risky innovations.

Table 29: (continued): HPI Low Score Configurations

			Impact of the Combination
	High	Learn. App.	Should seem bright, well informed, eager to learn, and willing to challenge others' ideas openly.
	Low	Learn. App.	Should seem argumentative and challenging while discounting the value of formal education.
Low Prudence	High	Inquisitive	Curious, thoughtful, and creative; open to new ideas and innovations; and willing to try new things.
	Low	Inquisitive	Tends to be impulsive, distractible, and disorganized but rarely reflects on the consequences of such behavior.
	High	Learn. App.	Will seem bright, well informed, interested in training, and willing to try new methods, techniques, and technology.
	Low	Learn. App.	Will seem impulsive, disorganized, and not interested in feedback.
Low Inquisitive	High	Learn. App.	Will seem smart and up to date but with little interest in innovations that lack a clear practical payoff.
	Low	Learn. App.	Will seem to lack curiosity or willingness to try anything new without personal experience regarding its utility.

Table 30: HPI High Score Configurations

		Impact of the Combination	
High Adjustment	High	Ambition	Calm, poised, self-confident, hardworking, upwardly mobile, somewhat aggressive, and eager to be in charge.
	Low	Ambition	Easygoing and self-satisfied; comfortable following rather than leading; seems to lack energy, passion, and drive.
	High	Sociability	Outgoing, talkative, self-confident, and entitled; expecting to be liked and accepted—nothing to prove.
	Low	Sociability	Quiet, self-confident, strong, silent type who will handle stress easily and without any noticeable drama.
	High	Inter. Sens.	Confident, friendly, relationship-oriented interpersonal style that creates a perception of modesty and inner strength.
	Low	Inter. Sens.	Will seem confident, self-assured, and perhaps arrogant with a direct, challenging, and blunt interpersonal style.
	High	Prudence	Hardworking, persistent, organized, dependable, mature, and very strong under stress and pressure.
	Low	Prudence	Calm and steady under pressure but disorganized and impulsive, sometimes creating havoc for others who have to fill in.
	High	Inquisitive	Curious, open minded, and able to generate new ideas with great confidence, often elevating them above the ideas of others.
	Low	Inquisitive	Confident, self-assured, and unflappable but with little interest in change, innovation, or enhanced understanding of current processes.
	High	Learn. App.	Bright, self-confident, well-informed, self-assured, and possibly arrogant but able to support opinions with logic and data.
	Low	Learn. App.	Self-confident, stable, and self-assured but perhaps smug and complacent, with little interest in acquiring new knowledge.

Table 30: (continued): HPI High Score Configurations

			Impact of the Combination
High Ambition	High	Sociability	Forceful, energetic, and hardworking; will communicate vigorously and reach out to others as a career development strategy.
	Low	Sociability	Quiet and reserved but intense and driven to succeed; will lead by example because action speaks louder than words.
	High	Inter. Sens.	Strong desires for achievement and success will be facilitated by real talent for building and maintaining relationships.
	Low	Inter. Sens.	Hardworking, competitive, and achievement oriented, combined with a blunt and challenging interpersonal style.
	High	Prudence	Unusually hardworking and achievement oriented, within a framework of conscientiousness and attention to detail.
	Low	Prudence	Competitive and achievement oriented, while regarding rules, processes, and procedures as barriers to be overcome.
	High	Inquisitive	Hardworking, achievement oriented, and leaderlike and a source for providing new ideas and vision.
	Low	Inquisitive	Hardworking and eager to succeed, but by doing something well and avoiding changes that may disrupt what is working.
	High	Learn. App.	Hardworking, competitive, and leaderlike but smart and up to date and will not suffer fools gladly.
	Low	Learn. App.	Hardworking and achievement oriented but impatient with training; strongly prefers to learn on the job.
High Sociability	High	Inter. Sens.	Gregarious, outgoing, and talkative but will be seen as warm, friendly, approachable, and charming.
	Low	Inter. Sens.	Good at starting relationships but will have trouble maintaining them due to their blunt interpersonal style.
	High	Prudence	Strong task orientation that will involve endless discussions of minute details in the name of accurate communication.
	Low	Prudence	Flexible, spontaneous, outgoing interactive style that may allow conversations to venture into gray or marginally appropriate areas.

Table 30: (continued): HPI High Score Configurations

			Impact of the Combination
	High	Inquisitive	Interested in meeting new people and exploring new ideas but might be regarded as lacking focus or easily distracted by the next new thing.
	Low	Inquisitive	Outgoing and approachable; primarily interested in the mundane or routine, with little interest in the big picture.
	High	Learn. App.	Smart and up to date with a breezy and approachable interpersonal style and quick to move on new and different topics.
	Low	Learn. App.	Gregarious, outgoing, and talkative but has little interest in current events or new developments in business or technology.
High Interpersonal Sensitivity	High	Prudence	Serious and conscientious; has high standards of performance but tolerant rather than self-righteous or picky.
	Low	Prudence	Pleasant, tolerant, and agreeable but with relatively low standards about timely and quality performance.
	High	Inquisitive	Cordial and pleasant, has a lively imagination, and willing to explore ideas regardless of how impractical they may be.
	Low	Inquisitive	Warm and engaging, has a rather prosaic imagination and little interest in the big picture.
	High	Learn. App.	Bright and well informed but does not flaunt their knowledge or criticize those who are less educated.
	Low	Learn. App.	Pleasant and sociable colleague with little interest in formal learning, current events, or new developments in technology.
High Prudence	High	Inquisitive	Strong interest in discussing ideas and innovation, with a tendency to be mired in the details during implementation.
	Low	Inquisitive	Strict adherence to rules, processes, and procedures, with little interest in innovation, particularly when things seem to be working.
	High	Learn. App.	Smart, well informed, hardworking, careful person with good judgment but reluctant to challenge established procedures.

Table 30: (continued): HPI High Score Configurations

	Impact of the Combination		
	Low	Learn. App.	Careful, conscientious, hardworking person with little interest in training and development; comfortable with what they already know.
High Inquisitive	High	Learn. App.	Bright, up to date, productive, and always on the lookout for new methods, technology, or paths to the future.
	Low	Learn. App.	Interested in new ideas and developments but prefers to hear about them and not read about them; open minded but intellectually lazy.

The HPI was constructed in a way that maximized the statistical independence of its seven scales. The independence of the HPI scales is what allowed us to develop Tables 29 and 30. However, the HDS and MVPI were developed based on content themes, and the scales are not statistically independent. This lack of statistical independence at the scale level makes providing a systematic method for configural interpretations of the three inventories taken together impossible. What follows is an ad hoc presentation of configural interpretations, but it should nonetheless be useful.

Personality and Careers

Certain configurations of scores on the three inventories are more appropriate to some career choices than others. But there are thousands of jobs in the world economy, each with its own optimal personality profile. How can we compare the personality requirements of different careers in a systematic way? This is where the Holland model becomes important (Gottfredson & Holland, 1996). The Holland model classifies jobs and occupations in terms of six robust categories (or types). The Holland system can classify every job in the Dictionary of Occupational Titles (DOT; Employment and Training Administration, U.S. Department of Labor, 1991). There are more than 12,000 specific occupations in the DOT, meaning that the Holland model is a comprehensive taxonomy of careers. See Table 31 for examples.

Realistic types tend to be characterized on the HPI by high Adjustment, Prudence, and Inquisitive scores and low Ambition and Learning Approach scores; such people are stable, reliable, and open minded. On the HDS, Realistic types are characterized by high Cautious, Reserved, and Diligent scores and low Colorful and Mischievous scores; such people seem tough, careful, meticulous, and predictable. On the MVPI, Realistic types receive high scores for Security, Tradition, and Science and low scores for Aesthetics, Hedonism, and Altruism. These people value stability, predictability, data-based decision-making, and self-reliance and have no time for frivolity—they can seem a bit dull.

Table 31: The Holland Model

Holland Type	Typical Jobs	Typical Requirements
Realistic	Engineer	Build, operate, maintain equipment.
	Computer scientist	Use equipment to solve problems.
	Medical doctor	Hands-on, practical applications.
	Building contractor	
	Airplane mechanic	
	Fireman/Policeman	
Investigative	Physicist	Gather and analyze data.
	Chemist	Find and solve problems.
	Mathematician	Explore the unknown.
	Biologist	
	Lab technician	
	Forensic analyst	
Artistic	Novelist/screen writer/poet	Create stories, designs, fantasies.
	Musician/Painter/Dancer	Decorate, embellish, fabricate images.
	Beautician	Entertain, amaze, and amuse others.
	Architect	
	Chef	
	Fashion designer	
Social	Counselor/therapist/teacher	Help, counsel, advise, teach others.
	Travel consultant	Serve and assist.
	Career coach	Guide and facilitate.
	Human resources specialist	
	Nurse	
	Athletic trainer	
Enterprising	Sales/Consulting	Solve business problems and advise people.
	Management/Supervision	Recruit staff and build support for projects.
	Entrepreneur/Investor	Find and evaluate business opportunities.
	Venture capitalist	
	Business owner	
	Sports promoter	
Conventional	Accounting and finance	Organize and manage data.
	Tax law and administration	Find and correct errors in the data.
	Computer scientist	Provide data to make operational decisions.
	Retail banking	
	Data scientist	
	Air traffic controller	

Investigative types, on the HPI, tend to receive very high Inquisitive, Learning Approach, Adjustment, and Ambition scores and low Prudence scores. Such people are seen as very bright and curious, creative, confident, and somewhat challenging/quarrelsome. On the HDS, Investigative types typically receive high Bold, Mischievous, Colorful, and Imaginative scores and low Diligent and Dutiful scores. Such people seem creative, assertive, challenging, and difficult to manage while testing limits. On the MVPI, Investigative types receive high Recognition, Power, Aesthetics, and Science scores and low Security and Hedonism scores. Such people value productivity, status, high-quality work, and close attention to details and are devoted to their craft—they can seem somewhat arrogant and aloof.

Artistic types, on the HPI, typically receive low Adjustment, Ambition, Sociability, Prudence, and Interpersonal Sensitivity scores and high Inquisitive scores. Such people seem creative, unorthodox, moody, disaffected, nonconforming, rude, and/or unsociable. On the HDS, Artistic types tend to receive high Reserved, Excitable, and Mischievous scores and low Bold and Dutiful scores. Such people tend to be irritable, socially remote, unassertive, careless about social obligations, and resentful of authority (even a bit delinquent). On the MVPI, Artistic types receive high Aesthetics and Altruism scores but low Science, Recognition, Affiliation, and Commerce scores. Such people value creative self-expression, intuitive problem-solving, and independence and are indifferent to fame and fortune—they can seem eccentric and unconventional.

Social types tend to receive high HPI scores for the Interpersonal Sensitivity, Sociability, and Learning Approach scales and low scores for the Adjustment, Ambition, Prudence, and Inquisitive scales. Such people seem not only smart, charming, and flexible but also modest and self-deprecating. On the HDS, Social types are characterized by high scores for the Excitable, Dutiful, and Leisurely scales and low scores for the Bold, Skeptical, and Dutiful scales. They will seem quiet, unassertive, hardworking, diplomatic, and pleasant. On the MVPI, Social types tend to receive high scores for the Altruistic and Aesthetics scales and very low scores for Tradition, Security, Commerce, and Science scales, suggesting that they will seem flexible, helpful, concerned about the welfare of the less fortunate, and prefer to make decisions based on feelings, not data—the typical Social type seems helpful, supportive, and tolerant.

Enterprising types tend to receive high scores on the HPI for the Interpersonal Sensitivity, Sociability, Ambition, and Learning Approach scales but low scores for the Prudence scale. Such people make strong and favorable first impressions and seem engaging, approachable, smart, flexible, confident, and leaderlike. The same is true for the HDS, where their scores suggest that Enterprising types seem energetic, outgoing, assertive, bold, adventurous, and risk-taking. On the MVPI, Enterprising types receive high scores for the Recognition, Commerce, and Hedonism scales but low scores for Tradition, Security, and Science scales, meaning that they want to be known, seen, and successful and have fun, with a passion for risk-taking and innovation and a preference for intuitive decision-making—they can take the oxygen out of a room.

Conventional types typically receive high scores on the HPI for Prudence and Learning Approach scales and low scores for the Sociability scale. Such people are seen as smart, well informed, socially appropriate, and somewhat introverted. On the HDS, Conventional types receive high scores for the Leisurely, Bold, Diligent, and Dutiful scales but low scores for the Mischievous and Imaginative scales. People with these scores will seem self-assured but pleasant, mannerly, and diplomatic. Loyal corporate citizens, they also seem very hardworking and careful about following rules and procedures. On the MVPI, Conventional types receive high scores for the Security, Tradition, and Commerce scales and low scores for the Affiliation, Altruism, and Hedonism scales. Such people are conservative, resist change, and are careful with money. Self-disciplined, they also tend to be somewhat remote, advocating self-reliance; they seem unconcerned about helping the disadvantaged. Note that Conventional types tend to have low scores for HPI Sociability and MVPI Affiliation scales, meaning that they seem introverted and socially remote—and perhaps lack social self-confidence. But Conventional types also have high scores for the HDS Bold scale, meaning that, beneath their socially remote exteriors, they are supremely self-confident, willing to take on tough assignments and challenge bad ideas. People may tend to underestimate them.

Syndrome Configurations

This discussion of configural interpretation requires a brief description of "syndrome" configurations. Syndromes are combinations of scales that predict a pattern of behavior that runs through a person's life. They help create a better understanding of people by recognizing the driving pattern of their personality and behavior. The following are some common examples.

Leading
High: HPI Ambition; MVPI Power
Moderate to High: HPI Inquisitive; HDS Bold

This pattern defines competitive people (Ambition) who enjoy being in charge and driving results (Power). They will be open to new ideas, offer new insights (Inquisitive), and be willing to take on challenging assignments (Bold).

Managing
High: HPI Ambition
Moderate to High: HPI Prudence; HDS Diligent; MVPI Altruism and Commerce

This pattern characterizes an upwardly mobile person (Ambition) who is conscientious about executing a business plan (Prudence) while being mindful of the details (Diligent), attentive to the bottom line (Commerce), and observant of their subordinates' needs (Altruism).

Creating
High: HPI Ambition and Inquisitive; HDS Imaginative; MVPI Aesthetics
Low: HPI Prudence

This pattern typifies energetic and driven people (Ambition) who are open to new ideas (Inquisitive), challenge conventional wisdom (low Prudence, high Imaginative), and are deeply concerned about issues of quality, taste, and style (Aesthetics).

Intimidating
High: HPI Ambition; HDS Reserved
Low: HPI Interpersonal Sensitivity and Sociability; MVPI Affiliation

This pattern characterizes aggressive people (Ambition) who are tough and insensitive (Reserved), blunt and abrasive (Interpersonal Sensitivity), socially remote (Sociability), and use silence as a weapon (Affiliation).

Ingratiating
High: HPI Sociability and Interpersonal Sensitivity; HDS Leisurely and Dutiful

This pattern typifies friendly and diplomatic people (Sociability and Leisurely) who avoid conflict (Interpersonal Sensitivity), willingly follow others' lead, try to be good corporate citizens, and seek the approval of management (Dutiful).

Resisting
High: HPI Prudence; HDS Leisurely, Cautious, and Diligent; MVPI Security
Low: HPI Inquisitive

This pattern of scores characterizes rigid, inflexible people (Prudence) who are stubborn and procrastinate (Leisurely), avoid making decisions (Cautious), fuss about details (Diligent), worry about changes that might threaten their status (Security), and resist change and innovation (Inquisitive).

Risk-Taking
High: HPI Sociability; HDS Mischievous
Low: HDS Cautious; HPI Prudence; MVPI Security and Tradition

An active and impulsive person who enjoys taking chances and seems unaffected by failure. Such people enjoy testing limits (Mischievous), view rules as obstacles to be overcome (Prudence), enjoy the role of risk-taker, and seek out environments that reward risk-taking (Security).

Diplomat
High: HPI Sociability and Interpersonal Sensitivity; HDS Cautious and Leisurely
Low: HPI Ambition; MVPI Power

These people pursue status by relying heavily on the ability to meet people and network (Sociability), build relationships (Interpersonal Sensitivity), avoid making mistakes (Cautious), and possibly being held accountable for results.

Perfectionist
High: HDS Diligent; MVPI Aesthetics and Science

These people have very high performance standards (Diligent); want to understand everything down to the slightest detail (Science); pay very close attention to details; care passionately about the look, feel, and quality of work products (Aesthetics); and are very hard to please (Diligent).

Summary

Using configural interpretation requires practice. The more you review HPI, HDS, and MVPI profiles, the better you will understand configural interpretations and value the results. The good news is that there is always something to learn as you study scores from these three inventories. The bad news is that providing a definitive guide to configural interpretation is not possible. The intent of this chapter was to help you think about configural interpretation. We provided some starting points, including dyadic interpretations on the HPI, key occupational clusters, and syndromes based on multiple scales on all three inventories. The interpretations of the six Holland types are a useful starting place in any interpretive process. They provide ideal profiles that can be compared with any specific profile. The differences between an ideal profile and one that you are reviewing will create an interesting, meaningful, and most of all, accurate interpretation.

Chapter 9
Conflict Interpretation

This guide has so far focused on interpreting common configurations within and across inventories. We now turn to configurations that entail apparent conflicts between scales. For example, how do we interpret a pattern of high Adjustment and Ambition and low Bold or high Ambition and Adjustment and very low Power? Seemingly conflicting results are common. This will be true when using (1) single inventories, where conflicts occur between scales; (2) multiple inventories, where conflicts occur across inventories; or (3) a combination of both situations.

Much can be learned from these conflicts, and they can be a significant source of concern in a person's life. Significant developmental benefit can be derived from these discrepancies when we understand them and how they are manifested behaviorally. Furthermore, people can improve their performance when they deal with the negative behaviors associated with these conflicts.

This chapter explores conflicting results from the inventories. We examine conflicts that occur within each inventory and then examine conflicts that arise between inventories. This is not a comprehensive review but, rather, an introduction to interpreting some conflicting results that we have observed.

HPI Conflicts

Conflicts between the scales on the HPI arise in two ways. First, different scales can yield similar behavioral descriptions. When a person is described as persistent, this may be the result of high Ambition (hardworking and upwardly mobile) or high Prudence (hardworking, good citizen). Two different HPI scales predict a high level of persistence.

Second, two scales that predict different behaviors occur together. For example, high Ambition (aggressive, competitive behaviors) seems to conflict with Interpersonal Sensitivity (diplomatic and tactful behavior). Thus, a manager with high scores on both scales may set high expectations for projects but avoid confronting others when they do not meet those expectations. These managers should feel conflicted; the conflict is real and may negatively impact job performance.

There are two more points about this. First, our personality inventories organize hundreds of behaviors into discrete, manageable units of analysis (i.e., scales and subscales). The inventories, in essence, reduce human variability to manageable proportions. Second, personality characteristics unpredictably combine to form new and interesting behaviors. The scales used to describe these characteristics will, at times, appear to complement and, at other times, contradict one another. Table 32 illustrates some common conflicts encountered within the HPI scales.

Table 32: Hogan Personality Inventory Conflicts

Conflict	Interpretation
Some scales override other scale results	
Low Adjustment	The negativity of low Adjustment often masks the tendencies of other scales.
High Ambition	High Ambition may compensate for the poor performance implications of, for example, low Prudence, but with frantic activity and poor time management.
High Sociability	High Sociability can briefly mask the poor performance implications of other scales—for example, during interviews.
High Prudence	High Prudence can mask the poor performance implications of other scales because of the task focus and added willingness to follow rules.
Behaviors That May Conflict Because of Scale Scores	
High Ambition and Low/High Adjustment	High Ambition with low Adjustment leads to intense, negative, exception-driven leadership; high Ambition with high Adjustment leads to goal-oriented leadership.
Opposites on Ambition and Sociability	High Ambition and low Sociability leads to high expectations and poor communication about goals; low Ambition and high Sociability results in frequent communication with no focus on goals.
High Ambition and High Interpersonal Sensitivity	High Ambition people are driven and competitive; high Interpersonal Sensitivity people are empathic and agreeable; it is difficult to be both a leader and a friend to subordinates.
Opposites on Sociability and Interpersonal Sensitivity	High Sociability and low Interpersonal Sensitivity lead to trying to socialize with people who want to avoid you; low Sociability and high Interpersonal Sensitivity results in avoiding people who want to interact, which makes you seem aloof.
High Prudence and High Inquisitive	High Prudence combined with high Inquisitive predicts being open to new ideas and able to see connections between unrelated pieces of information, but being too inflexible and detail oriented to change, innovate, or implement any new processes.

HDS Conflicts

Conflicts occur on the HDS when score elevations cross the super factors (Moving Away, Moving Against, and Moving Toward). For example, if a person has a strong Moving Away profile combined with a high score for Dutiful, that person's need for close alignment with superiors will conflict with their tendency to drive people away. Table 33 illustrates some common conflicts encountered with HDS results.

Table 33: Hogan Development Survey Conflicts

Conflict	Interpretation
Excitable and Leisurely	High scores on Excitable and Leisurely indicate that these people are easily upset (high Excitable) but are careful to keep their feelings to themselves (high Leisurely). So, others may see signs of stress but will rarely know the cause of the stress.
Cautious and Mischievous	High Cautious scores predict fear of failure and slow decision-making, whereas high Mischievous scores predict impulsivity and testing limits. Such people will seem careful and restrained, but the restraint is a facade. When they sense an opportunity and no one is watching, they will jump into projects with reckless abandon. They also tend to be stubborn about what they will do and how they will do it. Others will be annoyed with their inconsistent behavior and the hurry up/wait dichotomy.
Cautious and Dutiful	People with high scores on Cautious and Dutiful are often conflicted because they fear failure and hesitate to make decisions (Cautious); at the same time, they are eager to please their superiors (Dutiful), who are often in a hurry. The conflict between being careful and needing to hurry is intense and can inhibit successful job performance.
Reserved and Bold	People with high scores on Reserved are aloof, withdrawn, and interpersonally insensitive. When these tendencies are combined with arrogance and entitlement (high Bold), the result is a person who is tough, intimidating, demanding, and inflexible. That is, the person tends to intimidate subordinates, compete with peers, and show off for superiors.
Reserved and Colorful	People with high scores on Reserved and Colorful tend to be tough, insensitive, and socially remote (Reserved). At the same time, they seem to seek and need attention (Colorful). The result is that they use their odd interactional style to obtain attention while causing others confusion about how to deal with them.
Leisurely and Diligent	People with high Leisurely scores seem overtly pleasant but are covertly stubborn and independent. If they have high Diligent scores, they believe that there is one right way to do things and that their way is the only way. They (a) avoid being influenced by others, (b) quietly follow their own agendas, and (c) do not let others know what they are doing. This creates a reputation for being stubborn and a poor team player.

Table 33: (continued): Hogan Development Survey Conflicts

Conflict	Interpretation
Leisurely and Dutiful	People with high scores on these two scales are careful to avoid confrontations, especially with their seniors. People with high scores on Leisurely will agree to terms they find distasteful to reduce conflict and stress but will not follow through on their agreement. People with high scores on Dutiful will not challenge their boss (or popular positions) even when they disagree. As a result, they seem to be poor team players on whose support no one can depend.
Mischievous and Diligent	Mischievous is associated with reckless impulsivity (even delinquency), whereas Diligent is associated with very high standards of performance—and these are quite different tendencies. However, both concern being unwilling to follow rules other than their own. People with high scores on both scales seem independent, ready to ignore rules they find distasteful (Mischievous) while demanding that others conform to their personal rules and standards (Diligent). This is a common pattern among successful entrepreneurs and disrupters.

MVPI Conflicts

The MVPI scales reflect people's values. We rarely see people who are truly "conflicted" by their values. Rather than being conflicted, they usually want *both* values. For example, people with high Aesthetics and Science scores want work products to be *both* high functioning *and* stylish (high function and high form) as opposed to being conflicted about whether function or form is more important. A person with high Tradition and Hedonism scores might want to work in a culture that is conservative and buttoned down but *also* want to have lots of parties for employees.

Similarly, people with high Commerce scores are motivated to make money and can be selfish, whereas people with high Altruism scores are motivated to help others and are unselfish. Altruistic and Commerce seem incompatible, but some people receive high scores on both scales. Specifically, many entrepreneurs and venture capitalists (who have high Commerce scores) are quite altruistic—they want to make money in order to make a difference.

Repeating comments made earlier, the MVPI scales concern values, and this predicts two kinds of conflicts. On one hand, we like people who share our values, and we do not like people who do not—and this is a very robust generalization. For example, if one person has a high Tradition score and another has a low Tradition score, then they will not get along. On the other hand, every stable group has a culture defined by the group members' values. If a person's values are consistent with the dominant values of the group, then they will fit in. If, however, a person's values are inconsistent with the prevailing values of the group, then they will struggle to find a place in that group. These are the value conflicts that matter, and they concern the match between values between (not within) individuals.

Conflicts Between Inventories

Conflicts between inventories often yield valuable insights. As noted earlier, these conflicts predict behavioral patterns different from what we would expect based on the correlations between the scales across the three inventories.

Some conflicts create more tension than others. For example, people with low scores on the HPI Adjustment scale and high scores on the HDS Excitable scale may find controlling themselves difficult and may demonstrate an appropriate level of passion and urgency daily. In contrast, people with low scores for the HPI Sociability scale and high scores for the MVPI Affiliation scale may enjoy working quietly as a member of a highly visible team.

The following section describes some common conflicts that occur across the inventories. We highlight those that occur most frequently and may seem hard to interpret.

HDS Conflicts with the HPI

Excitable

People with high scores on the HDS Excitable scale typically receive low scores on the HPI Adjustment scale; such people are easily upset, which can lead to high Excitable behaviors, such as yelling at people. However, the self-critical tendencies associated with low Adjustment then cause them to worry about having yelled at people, even though they cannot seem to stop.

If people with high Excitable scores have high Adjustment scores, then look at the Ambition and Prudence scales of the HPI. People with high Ambition and Prudence scores tend to set high expectations for themselves and others, often exceeding the employees' capabilities. The result is that the boss yells (high Excitable) but thinks the staff deserves it (high Adjustment) for not meeting their expectations (high Ambition and Prudence). This behavior will stress employees.

Cautious

People with high scores on the HDS Cautious scale (risk avoidance) usually have high scores on the HPI Prudence (rule following) scale and low scores on the HPI Ambition (low aspirations) scale. Such people make slow decisions, avoid change, and are seen as bureaucrats.

If a person with high Cautious scores also has high Ambition scores, check their Adjustment score, which will likely be low. Such people have high performance expectations (high Ambition) but fear failure (low Adjustment) and tend to use fear as a motivator (e.g., "If we do not fix a, b, and c, we will all get fired"). Three things should be noted about this profile. First, many leaders have this high Cautious, high Ambition, low Adjustment profile. Second, fear-based motivation can produce short-term results. Finally, although fear-based motivation can succeed, working under these conditions is exhausting.

Diligent

People with high scores on the HDS Diligent scale usually have high scores on the HPI Prudence scale. But some people with high Diligent scores have low Prudence scores. Such people are relatively indifferent to (and may even challenge) standardized rules and procedures because they have their own (usually more demanding) rules and methods. However, under pressure, their Diligent tendencies can take over and turn into nitpicking and perfectionism.

Bold

People with high scores on the HDS Bold scale often have high scores on the HPI Adjustment scale. This combination predicts real arrogance and an inability to admit even minor faults and limitations. Such people also lack any sense of urgency, will not listen to feedback, and seem unable to learn from their mistakes—because they never acknowledge them.

Many people with high Bold scores and low scores on the HPI Adjustment scale are often high achievers (check the HPI Ambition and the MVPI Power scores). They are not only self-confident and willing to take on challenges but also have a need to prove themselves to others. They tend to work hard, solicit feedback on their performance, and learn from experience. This combination is often found in sales.

MVPI Conflicts with the HPI

While the MVPI concerns people's values and what they want in life, the HPI tells us about the behaviors people use to achieve what they want. Some people lack the personality characteristics (HPI) needed to achieve their goals (MVPI). When this happens, the conflicts are in the person, not the assessment. The following are the most commonly occurring conflicts.

Power and Ambition

People with high scores on the MVPI Power scale have high aspirations and plan their careers. People with high scores on the HPI Ambition scale tend to be driven, energetic, and competitive. We interpret people with low Power and high Ambition as "all sail and no rudder": Ambition concerns wanting to succeed; Power is about having a strategy to get there. People with low Power scores tend not to be strategic about their careers, which means their ambitions may be frustrated. People with high scores on the MVPI Power scale and low scores on the HPI Ambition scale are likely to be quite frustrated too—they want status but lack the personal resources to attain it.

Altruism and Interpersonal Sensitivity

People with high scores on the MVPI Altruism scale usually have high scores for the HPI Interpersonal Sensitivity scale. If, however, a person has a low Interpersonal Sensitivity score, then they want to help others (high Altruistic scores) but do so by giving them "tough love"—unvarnished feedback focused on the negative. People with low Altruism scores and high Interpersonal Sensitivity scores seem overtly kindly but are covertly indifferent to other people's needs.

Affiliation and Sociability

People with high scores on the MVPI Affiliation scale usually have high scores for the HPI Sociability scale. People with high Affiliation and low Sociability scores usually experience some tension between their desire for interaction and their remote, aloof interpersonal style. People with low Affiliation and high Sociability scores are energetic communicators who care little about actual social interaction; they are poor listeners who are happy communicating with strangers.

Security and Prudence

People with high scores on the MVPI Security scale usually have high scores on the HPI Prudence scale and vice versa. However, some people have high Security and low Prudence scores. This can be a problem because, although such people want to avoid risk, they are nonetheless impulsive and careless about rules. The reverse pattern—low Security and high Prudence—is much more functional; such people enjoy innovation and risk-taking (low Security) but will do so in a planned, organized (high Prudence) manner.

HDS and MVPI Conflicts

Conflicts between the HDS and the MVPI occur when people have goals that will be difficult to attain because their personality characteristics inhibit their attainment. The following are examples of these types of conflicts.

Power and Bold

People with high scores on the MVPI Power scale want to get ahead in life. Courage and confidence (HDS Bold) will enhance their chances of success. However, if they are also arrogant and unable to learn from experience (high HDS Bold scores), then they will alienate the people whose support they need in order to succeed. People with high scores on the MVPI Power scale but low scores on the HDS Bold scale want to lead and achieve but may be too hesitant and risk-averse to pursue their ambition.

Altruistic and Reserved

People with high scores on MVPI Altruism and HDS Reserved scales are likely to be conflicted because, although they want to help others (Altruistic), they are unable personally to engage them (high Reserved). Consequently, the person being helped may not appreciate it regardless of the other person's intentions.

Security and Mischievous

People with high scores on the MVPI Security scale typically have low scores on the HDS Mischievous scale. People with high Security scores who also have high Mischievous scores tend to be mischief-makers who enjoy testing limits, defying authority, and stirring things up, but they do this in ways that are difficult to detect.

Summary

This chapter described some interpretation conflicts that you are likely to encounter when using the three inventories. In many ways, the most important challenge when interpreting inventory results is to be able to explain scale results that seem to conflict. Results that appear to conflict are unavoidable. Sometimes, these conflicts have little impact on understanding the results. Other times, the impact can be quite profound. By recognizing and effectively interpreting conflicting results, you will be able to add significant value in understanding the inventories' results.

Chapter 10
Feedback: The Hogan Way

Thus far, we have addressed scale definitions, interpretations, and configurations. In the next two chapters, we turn our focus to applying the Hogan results to feedback and coaching sessions to maximize their impact on the leader's effectiveness. At Hogan, we view the assessment–feedback–coaching process as the "what," the "so what," and the "now what." The scales scores are the "what" (what behaviors am I likely to demonstrate), the feedback session is the "so what" (so what do these scores mean for me as a leader), and the coaching sessions are the "now what" (now what do I do to be a more effective leader). We have covered the "what" in previous chapters, so in the following two chapters, we cover the "so what" and the "now what." Routinely, leaders advise us that this process of

- taking an assessment that results in valid and accurate data;

- receiving feedback from an expert who provides meaningful insights into key strengths, development needs, values, and blind spots; and

- participating in coaching with a seasoned professional who helps them identify specific actions to take to become more effective is impactful and even life-changing.

Thus, the next two chapters will not teach how to provide feedback or how to coach, as we assume the reader will rely on their already well-honed feedback and coaching skills. Rather, we will share the "Hogan Way" of feedback and coaching, which leverages the unique data provided by the Hogan assessments to achieve maximum impact—turning insights into action.

The feedback session is where the Hogan results start to "live and breathe" in the leader's life. It is the opportunity for the coach and the leader to discuss the "so what" of the leader's results: So, what do these scale scores mean for my effectiveness? How do I show up on a day-to-day basis? What are the possible impacts on my team and coworkers? The feedback session lays the foundation for the "now what" (now what do I do) and action planning covered in subsequent coaching sessions. This chapter does not concern how to give feedback, as experience is the best teacher. Rather, it concerns tips for delivering meaningful feedback that have been identified by members of the Hogan Coaching Network (HCN), Hogan's cadre of experienced professionals who have conducted thousands of feedback sessions.

The Goal of Feedback

The goal of feedback is to increase a person's strategic self-awareness in the service of enhanced personal effectiveness, team performance, and business results.

Providing high-quality feedback is a balance between art (the ability of a skilled coach to orchestrate the feedback) and science (the technical validity of the Hogan inventories).

It requires the coach to analyze, interpret, and integrate the Hogan data to provide meaningful insights regarding key strengths, areas for development, values, and blind spots. From these insights, a dynamic discussion between the coach and the leader results in key takeaways that will have the greatest positive impact on the leader's effectiveness. These takeaways lay the groundwork for specific development-related action items created in subsequent coaching sessions.

Advice from the Pros

The following advice from HCN coaches highlights key topics commonly encountered during feedback sessions and offers proven practices for creating a meaningful experience for the leader:

I. Prepare for the Session

II. Select the Feedback Approach

III. Establish the Frame

IV. Leverage Hogan's Foundational Concepts

V. Simplify and Clarify

VI. Encourage New Perspectives

VII. Demonstrate Strong Coaching Skills

I. Prepare for the Session

Solid preparation is a hallmark of a successful feedback session. This is where the integration of art and science begins, as the coach needs to review the data for insights (science) and think through the best way to position the feedback with the leader (art). We recommend that you do the following:

1. Learn all you can about the leader. For feedback sessions associated with a leadership development initiative, many times you will have the leader's resume or recent 360 survey results, which can provide critical insights into their experience (resume) and observations from their current work group (360). If the feedback session is standalone, obtaining background information is more difficult, and coaches often turn to publicly available information, such as a professional profile.

2. Review and analyze the leader's Flash Report not only for significant scales and common themes to include in the discussion but also to determine how apprehensive and/or accepting the leader might be of the feedback. If the leader has a low score on the No Hostility subscale of Interpersonal Sensitivity and a low score on the Not

Anxious subscale of Adjustment, they will likely be more reticent during the session, something you will need to account for. Similarly, leaders with high scores on Adjustment might not accept feedback; knowing this can guide your approach.

3. Think about your own Hogan results and how you might need to modify your style to accommodate the leader's style. If the leader has a low score on Sociability, they might be overwhelmed by a high Sociability coach, and the coach will need to dial this down.

4. Make a list of major takeaways arising from the common themes to have in your back pocket at the end of the session. You should ask the leader what their major takeaways are. If the leader struggles or overlooks something, you can use the list for suggestions to the leader.

II. Select the Feedback Approach

While there are numerous ways to give feedback, we describe the three most common approaches:

- **The Thematic Approach**

  Coaches find that identifying common themes across multiple assessments is especially powerful for leaders. This involves "skipping around" somewhat between the HPI, the HDS, and the MVPI, but if explained clearly, the leader will not be confused. Identifying themes early in the session allows the coach to build on them throughout the discussion. For example, if a leader has high scores on the Ambition (HPI), Bold (HDS), and Power (MVPI) scales, the coach can introduce the theme of being confident and results oriented when discussing the HPI. Then the coach may move to the HDS and the MVPI to tie in Bold and Power. The coach might say something like:

  Your high Ambition score shows that you're likely confident, results oriented, and leader-like. This is reinforced by the Bold scale on the HDS and the Power scale on the MVPI. Your high Ambition is key to your success; however, you might overuse it at times, and high Bold will appear—coming on too strong or being perceived as arrogant. This confident/results-oriented theme is also borne out by your high Power score that suggests you'll create a culture of accountability and value high-impact contributions.

The thematic approach helps leaders "connect the dots" much more rapidly than a linear, assessment-based approach to feedback (described next), where the coach covers the HPI, the HDS, and the MVPI individually. It also saves time because the coach does not have to repeat, "Remember what we said about your Ambition score a few minutes ago? Well, here's another side to it in your high Bold."

The thematic approach also assists in making development themes and their impact readily identifiable at the end of the session because the coach and the leader have discussed the theme throughout.

- **The Assessment-Based Approach**

The assessment-based approach is the simplest feedback structure and is organized around the three Hogan inventories. This feedback structure starts with the HPI or the MVPI and progresses through each inventory, scale by scale (typically covering every scale for the HPI and the highest and lowest scales for the HDS and the MVPI), and builds a complete picture of strengths and opportunities. This feedback structure builds meaning from the information blocks. For newer coaches, this is the easiest form of feedback to deliver because it is the most linear of the three structures presented here. The benefits of the assessment-based approach include that it is clear, can be quick, and is easy to manage. The downside of this structure is that developing robust themes may be harder, and nuances that would help identify developmental opportunities may be missed.

- **The Specific Need Approach**

This approach structures the feedback session to address a specific, pre-identified need that was the impetus for the leader's taking the Hogan inventories and perhaps participating in subsequent coaching. The pre-identified need is typically related to competencies required for a specific job or a particular issue or challenge confronting a leader. For example, if the leader's job requires strong strategic skills, and the leader is more operational, then the feedback approach would focus on the scales associated with strategic thinking. Or, if a leader did everything themselves and needed to delegate more to their team, the approach would focus on scales related to delegation. When the coach is working with a leader on a very specific issue, the coach can use the Hogan results to focus closely on it and customize the feedback to address it. In this approach, while the feedback will usually cover all the HPI scales and many of the HDS and MVPI scales, the coach is going to great lengths to specifically address the ways the leader's Hogan data inform their developmental needs. Whatever the specific need, this approach tailors the Hogan feedback to it.

III. Establish the Frame

Typically, a feedback session is scheduled for 60 or 90 minutes. Given the wealth of information in the Hogan data, covering all aspects in such a short time is difficult. The most successful coaches make sure they have a structure in place to help them manage their time. A clear, cohesive framework helps ensure that the purpose and goals of the feedback are clear and, perhaps even more importantly, that the leader feels safe while hearing the feedback. The frame also helps organize the high volume of data so that the leader can focus on what is most important. With a clear, solid frame, the leader knows what to expect and is better able to focus on their development. Included at the end of this chapter is a step-by-step explanation of Hogan's feedback framework. While the elements of the feedback framework can take place simultaneously, they are discussed separately in the model for clarity. Furthermore, the following tips and suggestions from coaches can be applied throughout the feedback framework, depending on when the subject arises.

IV. Leverage Hogan's Foundational Concepts

Several concepts set Hogan apart from other assessment companies. Coaches find that in many cases, these are new concepts for the leader receiving feedback, and these can provide a new perspective for the leader when considering and acting on their assessment results. Coaches make sure they cover these concepts at some point in the feedback discussion:

1. Personality matters tremendously in leadership. At Hogan, we say, "Who you are determines how you lead." Often, leaders view their results through their personal lens only, and understanding this concept prompts them to view their results through the lens of their role as a leader.

2. There is a difference between identity and reputation. Identity is "the you that you know," and reputation is "the you that others know." For many leaders, these are at odds. As Hogan practitioners, we know that "reputation is the most consequential aspect of personality and is what organizations, teammates, and/or partners use to evaluate our effectiveness." By familiarizing leaders with this concept and the unique way the Hogan assessments measure personality, we can help leaders understand and accept the assessment data.

3. Strategic self-awareness is of paramount importance. To be effective, leaders must be aware of their strengths, areas for development, blind spots, values, and how they compare to others. Once aware, they can do something about them.

4. Context, or situational awareness, is the partner of strategic self-awareness. The leader's context has a huge impact on how to interpret their Hogan results, as far as what could be a strength and what could be something to watch out for. Coaches should make it clear early in the session that there is no such thing as a "good" or "bad" scale score—it is context dependent. In fact, context is what distinguishes feedback (explaining a leader's scale scores and providing the definition of the scale) and *development* feedback (putting the scores in the leader's context and identifying what they can do to be more effective).

5. Your personality is not your destiny. Even though a leader's personality is not easily changed, they can change their behavior through intentional development, thereby impacting their reputation.

6. Hogan defines leadership not by where a leader sits in the hierarchy but by the ability to build, maintain, and motivate a team that outperforms the competition. Coaches find that sharing this with leaders (who have direct reporting teams) encourages

them to think about their Hogan results in terms of the effect on their team and broader stakeholder groups. This shifts the lens from the leader only to their impact on others.

V. Simplify and Clarify

It is imperative that the leader who is receiving feedback not be overwhelmed and confused by the different purposes of the three inventories and the number of scales and subscales. Coaches find keeping explanations and descriptions as clear as possible crucial. Often, this involves simplifying verbiage and descriptions. As they deliver more feedback sessions, coaches develop approaches to simplify the data and develop "elevator speech" versions of explanations. The following are some of their well-proven methods:

- **Use a Funnel Approach**

  - Because of the volume of information provided by the assessments, a funnel approach is recommended to present information about scales. This approach helps convey information about the scales with clarity, starting with the general and progressing to more specific, personal, and contextualized interpretations.

  - The coach begins by defining and describing the scale, followed by incorporating the leader's context and relevant subscales into the interpretation, and then integrating several scales to enhance meaning, and culminating in the development of a trend or theme. This process is shown in Figure 1.

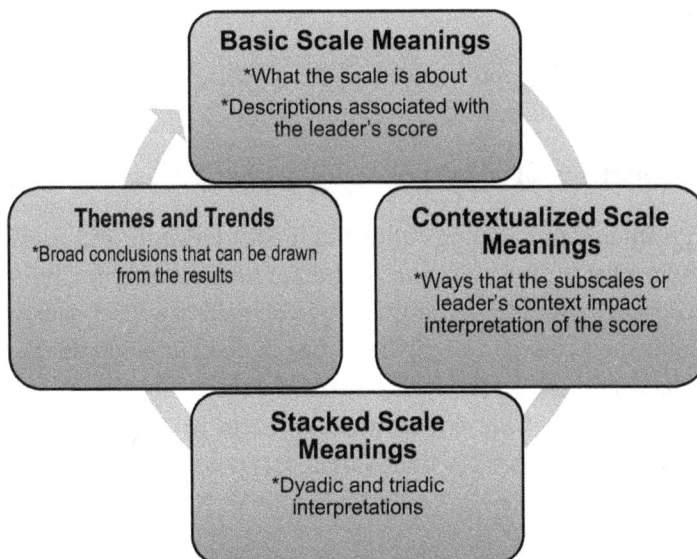

Figure 1 The Funnel Approach to Hogan Feedback

- **Overview the HPI, the HDS, and the MVPI in elevator speech versions—the terms *bright side*, *dark side*, and *inside* help leaders understand the differences between the inventories.**

  - Hogan Personality Inventory—The HPI concerns the "bright side" of personality. It describes how others see you when you are at your best. If we asked those who know you well to describe you, they would most likely describe you in a way that is consistent with your HPI results. The HPI identifies your key strengths. It is a predictor of the day-to-day reputation you have.

  - Hogan Development Survey—The HDS concerns "the dark side" of personality. It describes how others see you when you are not paying attention to your performance—when you are not self-monitoring—and this leads to performance risks. These performance risks emerge when your guard is down—when you are stressed, tired, or comfortable with those around you—and when these risks appear, others notice and remember them.

  - Motives, Values, Preferences Inventory—The MVPI concerns the "inside" of personality. It identifies what you value and what motivates you. It provides an indication of how well aligned you will feel with a job, career, or organization. When alignment is high, you will be happy and energized; when alignment is low, the opposite will occur. The MVPI is also a predictor of the kind of culture you will create as a leader and the unconscious biases you might have (e.g., what behaviors you naturally encourage or discourage).

- **Reinforce understanding with an alternative description of the HPI, the HDS, and the MVPI if needed.**

  - Think of the MVPI as "what you want," the HPI as "what will get you there," and the HDS as "what will get in your way."

- **Emphasize the importance of context in deciding what will have the greatest impact.**

  - Given the large amount of data, the context of the leader's role and goals can guide them to focus on what is most relevant for them. The session is about the leader, not the coach, so coaches should request that the leader share a brief background—for example, What is their role? How long have they been in it? What do they consider their key strengths and areas for development? What are their key business and leadership challenges? How big is their team, and how would they describe their current functioning? and What are their career aspirations?

- **Identify the situations that evoke conflicting scales.**

  - Sometimes leaders are confused by their scores on conflicting scales, and they ask, "Aren't these the opposite of each other?" Many times, their behaviors are indeed the opposite of each other, and they are brought out by different situations. Coaches find that helping the leader identify the situations that evoke the respective behaviors provides clarity. For example, if a leader has high scores on both the Cautious and the Mischievous scales, it might be that they are cautious when they are faced with a challenge they have never dealt with before (they advise the group, "We'd better slow down and think this over"), but they are mischievous if they have successfully dealt with the challenge in the past (they encourage the group, saying, "C'mon, let's just do it").

VI. Encourage New Perspectives

An important part of increasing strategic self-awareness is to encourage the leader to look at their behaviors through a different lens. Coaches have found that describing results in a different way sometimes prompts this. The following are some tips on how to do this:

- **HDS scales as coping styles**

  - HDS scales are typically described in terms of derailers, but often, the fact is that they are coping styles that may be not serving them. Coaches should point this out, as it can help the leader identify with the derailer and how it unfolds for them.
  - Sometimes leaders fail to understand that there is a positive side to HDS scales that, when overused, can result in performance risks. They can be a valuable part of a leader's repertoire if they are not overused or underused. There is a "sweet spot."

- **The MVPI is a predictor of the kind of culture the leader will create.**

  - An important but sometimes overlooked aspect of the MVPI is that it predicts the kind of culture the leader will create. This can be a real "aha" moment for leaders who have never thought about their values as determinants of this.

- **Use subscales to provide clarity and nuance.**

  - While feedback should focus on the major scales, coaches should use the subscales if they provide clarity or nuance. Using subscales can be particularly helpful when a leader says they do not relate to the behaviors indicated by the scales. Many times, they will relate to a subscale, or the subscale pattern will explain why the main scale interpretation may not resonate.

VII. Demonstrate Strong Coaching Skills

Successful feedback sessions involve bringing together science and art in a meaningful way. The science is the Hogan data interpretation skills; the art is the skills of the coach. Here are the skills HCN coaches have identified as most important:

1. Being supportive, collaborative, and nonjudgmental. The coach needs to encourage the leader to participate and share their stories and thoughts so the data can be connected to their real-world experiences.

2. Good verbal skills, including the ability to build rapport, engage the leader in dialogue, and convey complex ideas in a clear, compelling manner. Additionally, the coach needs to be able to create powerful questions. Questions can sometimes be the best tool to help leaders connect Hogan data to their lived experiences. Questions fostering this connection are not necessarily brilliant, clever, or well spoken; rather, they need to hit the core of the leader's experiential world and open the possibility that the experience is related to the scale score.

3. Good listening skills to hear what is being said beyond the stories and examples to the essential meanings. The coach must be able to attune to a wide variety of leaders.

4. Ability to connect the multiple data points in the Hogan inventories (and multi-rater assessments, prior development plans, etc., if available) into a story and then interpret the data while considering what the leader presents as their history and ability to understand the feedback. There is a unifying meaning under the sheer amount of all the information. The coach needs to be able to find that meaning.

5. Flexibility and ability to think on their feet. This is true not only in the sense of shifting interpretations as the leader presents information but also in the sense of the coach's ability to shift their feedback style to meet the leader's learning style and personality characteristics.

6. Ability to tolerate ambiguity and contain a wide variety of emotional reactions from leaders.

Insights into Action

A well-orchestrated feedback session conducted the Hogan Way ensures that the leader leaves the session with insights that they can turn into specific actions to have a major positive impact on their effectiveness. If the leader continues with coaching sessions, the coach can assist in adding details, identifying measures, and defining success. If the leader does not proceed with coaching sessions, they can still add specificity to their takeaways in a development plan they create with their manager or human resources partner to enhance their leadership effectiveness.

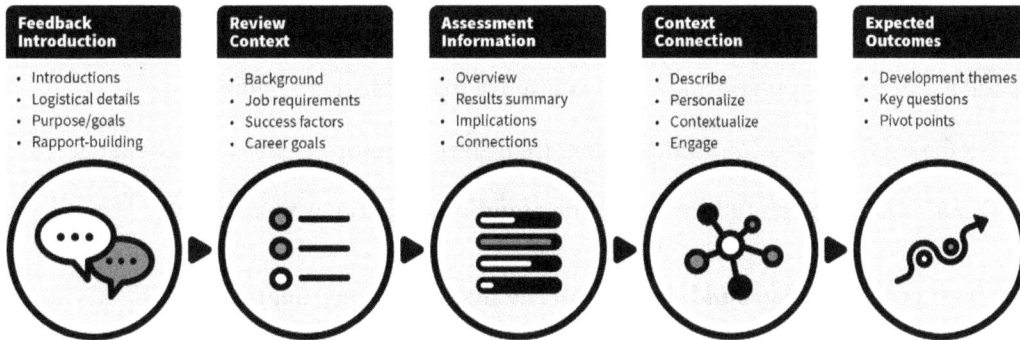

Figure 2 Hogan's Feedback Framework

Overview of the Feedback Framework

The feedback framework model (Figure 2) consists of five parts: Feedback Introduction, Review Context, Assessment Information, Context Connection, and Expected Outcomes. Each part is reviewed next.

Feedback Introduction: Details, Purpose, Expectations, and Rapport

Leaders often come to a feedback session having no idea what to expect. The coach should review some basic parameters with the leader to ensure alignment, pace the session, and build trust. In the Feedback Introduction, the coach should review the details, purpose, and expectations while building rapport with the leader. The following are a few examples of what to cover:

Details

- Length of session

- Confidentiality of information

- How the assessment information will be used

Purpose

- Increase strategic self-awareness to enhance the leader's effectiveness

Expectations

- Identify a few major takeaways (strengths to leverage, things to watch out for to rein in, etc.) that, if improved, would significantly increase the leader's effectiveness.

- Ask what the leader's expectations are.

Rapport

- Tell a little about yourself and your experience to establish credibility.

- Ask the leader to provide context about themselves, their role, and their challenges.

- Be curious, listen carefully, reflect understanding, and show empathy.

Review Context: Background, Job Requirements, and Career Goals

Coaches might debrief a wide variety of leaders from a wide variety of situations. While accurately interpreting Hogan scales without information about situational context is possible, much of the developmental richness of Hogan data is lost without this information. The leader's history and experiences help the coach understand the way scale-related behaviors may show up in the real world, now and in the future. Leveraging the components of Review Context provides an opportunity for the coach to do this. Time may not permit a lengthy discussion about context, but at a minimum, the coach should ask about several of the following:

Background

- Career history

- Education and training

- Work experience

Job Requirements

- Current role demands and CSFs (critical success factors)

- Team context (if the leader has a team)

- Challenges the leader is facing

Career Goals

- Current and future career objectives

- Professional (and personal, if appropriate) goals

Assessment Information: Introduction, Overview, Integration, and Questions

Once the frame has been set and context parameters have been discussed, moving to the Assessment Information step to provide an overview of the Hogan assessments is important. This is especially important because the Hogan tools are quite different from commonly used assessments, and a clear explanation up front saves time, reduces confusion, and sets the groundwork for more accurate interpretations of the data.

Introduction

- Establish credibility of the Hogan tools.

- Briefly explain assessment foundations (scientifically validated; developed for workplace assessment).

- Outline what the Hogan assessments measure (normal personality).

Overview

- Describe the HPI, the HDS, and the MVPI and what they measure in elevator speech terms (covered earlier in this chapter).

Integration

- Explain how the assessments interact and nuance each other.

- Identify common themes across the assessments.

Questions

- Ask if the leader has any questions before you begin your deep dive.

- Ask what their initial reaction is to their results—any surprises?

NOTE: *For a 60-minute feedback session, the feedback introduction, review context, and assessment information components should take no longer than 12–15 minutes.*

Context Connection: Describe, Contextualize, Integrate, and Engage

- The coach is now ready to move to the actual interpretation of the results. Because of the volume of information, a funnel approach is recommended to present information about the scales. This approach helps convey information about the scales with clarity, starting with the general and progressing to more specific, personal, and contextualized interpretations.

Describe

- Explain scale definitions—cover all HPI scales, high and very low scores on HDS scales, and high MVPI scales.

- Describe performance implications.

Contextualize

- Explore how context influences score interpretation by making connections between Hogan data and the leader's context, goals, and job requirements.

- Ask whether the interpretation connects to the recipient's experience.

Integrate

- Identify themes and trends across multiple assessments.

- Use stacked scales—dyadic and triadic scale combinations.

Engage

- Keep the leader engaged by asking questions and checking with the leader for whether the feedback resonates.

- Make sure this is a two-way dialogue.

NOTE: *For a 60-minute feedback session, the Context Connection component should take about 35–40 minutes.*

Expected Outcomes: Development Goals, Pivot Points, Next Steps, and Close

- At this point, the coach has created a research-based, yet personalized and contextualized understanding and interpretation of the Hogan data. So what?

Development Goals

- Identify key takeaways, trends, and development themes.

- Prioritize these to address the ones that will be most impactful for the leader's performance, and turn these into development goals (typically 2 to 3).

Pivot Points

- Identify pivot points—places where the leader can make small shifts from ineffective behaviors and pivot toward more appropriate behaviors.

Next Steps

- If the leader has coaching sessions scheduled, explain that during the next session, you will identify actions they can take to support achievement of their development goals; ask the leader to identify action items as homework.

- If coaching sessions are not ensuing, ask the leader to identify actions on their own, have a discussion with their manager, and create a development plan.

Close

- Ask the leader if they have any further questions or concerns.

- Offer further support as appropriate.

- Thank them for their time.

NOTE: *For a 60-minute feedback session, the Expected Outcomes component should take about 10–12 minutes.*

Chapter 11
Coaching the Hogan Way

Leadership development continues to be at the top of organizations' agendas due to the significant difference leadership makes to results across all categories, including financial metrics, customer satisfaction, employee satisfaction, and employee engagement. Executive coaching has become a centerpiece in many leadership development initiatives because the business world has finally caught up to the sports, health, and fitness industries in realizing the following:

- Coaching works.

- Coaching is a performance lever, not a last-ditch intervention.

- Coaching is equally necessary for Most Valuable Players and rookies.

- Coaching provides unmatched opportunities for feedback, insight, and accountability.

Just as elite athletes such as Olympians, footballers, tennis pros, and others rely on coaches to help them maximize their potential, leaders and senior executives are harnessing the power of professional coaching to "up their game."

Leadership Development Is Broken!

At Hogan, we believe leadership development is broken! We have identified seven common shortfalls (Kellett & Sahm, 2024) in leadership development that contribute to its "brokenness":

- Defining leadership incorrectly

- Measuring circular outcomes

- Chasing moving targets

- Taking a "one size fits all" approach to development

- Overlooking the importance of context

- Neglecting the psychology of behavior change

- Decoupling assessment and development activities

To fix leadership development, we need to address the seven shortfalls and replace them with working solutions. Hogan coaching does exactly that by leveraging Hogan assessment data and years of experience working with leaders. The seven shortfalls and Hogan's solutions are shown in Table 34.

Table 34: Shortfalls in Leadership Development and Hogan Solutions

Shortfall in Leadership Development	Hogan Solution
Defining leadership incorrectly	Redefine leadership
Measuring circular outcomes	Measure relevant outcomes
Chasing moving targets	Refocus on steady targets
Taking a "one size fits all" approach to development	Leverage individual differences via assessment data
Overlooking the importance of context	Treat context as paramount
Neglecting the psychology of behavior	Change is hard; make it easier
Decoupling assessment and development activities	Fix the broken link between assessment and development activities

In this chapter, we explain each solution in greater detail. We also demonstrate how each solution is addressed by Hogan coaching.

This chapter does not aim to teach people how to coach. Just as in the previous chapter, we assume the reader was a proficient feedback provider, and we assume the reader is an experienced coach who is proficient in coaching techniques such as the following:

- Putting the leader at ease

- Creating a safe space for open discussion

- Honoring confidentiality

- Being nonjudgmental

- Practicing superior listening skills

- Asking pertinent questions

- Inspiring reflection

- Using behavior- and evidence-based coaching

- Supporting the leader

- Challenging the leader when needed

- Encouraging learning and behavior modification

- Creating a development plan with metrics to measure progress

- Holding the leader accountable

- Possessing an expansive coaching "toolkit" that includes materials, models, exercises, readings, and the like that can be customized to the leader's needs

Leadership Development Shortfalls and Hogan Solutions

We will now look at the seven shortfalls in greater detail and how Hogan coaching counteracts them:

Element 1
Shortfall: Defining Leadership Incorrectly
Hogan Solution: Redefine Leadership

At Hogan, we believe the traditional definition of leadership is wrong. Historically, leadership has been defined by a person's position in an organization's hierarchy. Regardless of whether a person was effective, they were considered a "leader" based on their position. Hogan defines leadership not by the position a person holds but as the ability to build, maintain, and motivate a team that outperforms the competition. Furthermore, we view leadership as a resource for the group, not as a source of privilege for the incumbent.

When organizations ignore this team component of leadership, it can result in leaders being promoted solely based on their social presence. They might be successful until their lack of team leadership skills becomes obvious in a critical position, and they stumble, bringing the team down with them. This occurrence happens so often that it has a name: "The Peter Principle."

Hogan coaching takes this new definition of leadership into account by addressing the impact of the leader's strengths, development needs, and blind spots not only on their own performance but also on their team's well-being and performance. Hogan coaching shifts the lens so that the leader gleans insights into their impact on their team and their team's ability to perform effectively.

Often, a person must lead a team that is not composed of their direct reports, such as a cross-functional initiative or an ad hoc team. Regardless of reporting relationships, the person is still the leader and needs to view success through a team lens rather than an individual lens.

Element 2
Shortfall: Measuring Circular Outcomes
Hogan Solution: Measure Relevant Outcomes

Too often, leadership development initiatives and executive coaching focus on outcomes that are "circular" or that are too narrow. Consistent with our view that leadership is all about followership, we believe outcomes should be focused on the team's performance, not merely on the leader's performance. Typically, the success of leadership development programs is measured at their conclusion primarily by leader-centric measures such as the following:

- Did the leader like the program?

- Did the leader get promoted?

- Did the leader evaluate their progress positively in a subjective self-rating?

- Did the leader score well on performance ratings after the program?

These measures lead to circular outcomes because they are either self-evaluations by the leader or they point to the same one or two people who evaluate the leader.

At Hogan, we believe these circular feel-good goals need to be replaced by specific measurable criteria that are relevant to development, such as the following:

- Did the leader set actionable, relevant **change goals** that positively impacted the team?

- Did the leader **take action** on these goals following the program?

- Did any measure of **team effectiveness improve** following the program?

- Did the leader show any **improvement in post-program 360 scores**?

In short, our evaluation of the coaching initiative's success is team focused and other focused rather than merely leader focused or contaminated by organizational politics.

Element 3
Shortfall: Chasing Moving Targets
Hogan Solution: Refocus on Steady Targets

Many times, leadership development initiatives, including coaching, focus on moving targets such as fads, buzzwords, books, human resources (HR) crazes, or leadership competency models. The problem with competency models, no matter how well researched, is that they lead to the black-and-white style of thinking that a leader either has or does not have a competency. This leads to conclusions that the presence of a competency is "good" and the absence of one is "bad," that "more is better," and other fallacious judgments.

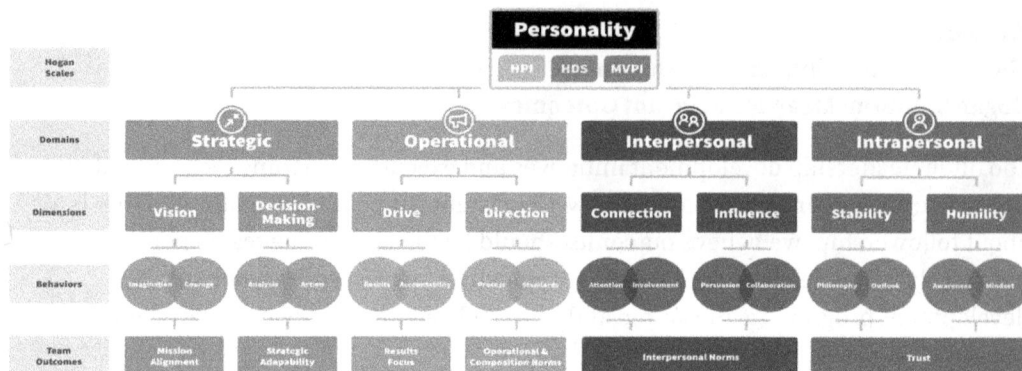

Figure 3 The Hogan Leadership Model

At Hogan, we believe the competency model approach oversimplifies leadership. To address this, we created the Hogan Leadership Model (see Figure 3), a well-researched and statistically valid model correlated with scales from the three Hogan assessment instruments. As depicted in Figure 3, our model is based on four universal domains that demand a leader's time and attention. There are two dimensions under each domain (8 total dimensions) and two behaviors under each dimension (16 total behaviors). The Hogan Leadership Model does not judge *if* a leader has a competency but rather *how* a behavior unfolds. The model is context based, allowing for nuanced interpretation.

Hogan coaching focuses on the four domains and the associated dimensions and behaviors that are foundational to leadership. Furthermore, we focus on *how* the leader approaches the domains and exhibits the behaviors, not on *if* they do so, so we avoid the traditional polarized thinking of *have* or *have not*. Because context is all-important, we tailor our coaching targets (behavior modifications and skill acquisition) to the leader's unique situation and to the needs of the team.

When a client has a leadership or competency model that the client wants the Hogan coach to use as a framework, we can do so. However, we still take the approach of *how* a behavior is demonstrated, not *if* it is demonstrated.

Element 4
Shortfall: Taking a "One Size Fits All" Approach to Development
Hogan Solution: Leverage Individual Differences via Assessment Data

A core Hogan belief is "who you are determines how you lead." Therefore, a leader's personality that reveals *who* they are is crucial in determining *how* they will lead. Leaders and their personalities are unique, and one size *does not* fit all. Individual differences in strengths, watchouts, and blind spots need to be identified and addressed in any development process.

Leadership development initiatives that fail to recognize one size does not fit all can result in a leader overusing a strength they are already competent in. This can make the leader less effective, which defeats the purpose of the leadership development initiative. For instance, one leader who was strong in strategic thinking was sent to a "cookie cutter" leadership development program with a strategic thinking module. They excelled in the program, but subsequently, they ended up being less effective because they overused an already developed strength. They and their team would have been much better served by the leader attending a module addressing a strength they needed to develop.

Assessment data are a critical diagnostic tool for a coach to use. Not having assessment data as a foundation is similar to a doctor prescribing medicine without establishing the root causes of the patient's issue. All Hogan coaching initiatives begin with the administration of the HPI, the HDS, and the MVPI, which reveal the uniqueness of the leader's personality. Even if two leaders have the same score on a scale, they will not necessarily behave the same way due to having different subscale scores or the way the scale interacts with other scales. Identifying this uniqueness helps highlight the most impactful areas to address with coaching. Assessments also provide a baseline against which the leader can be compared later to determine the initiative's success.

Element 5
Shortfall: Overlooking the Importance of Context
Hogan Solution: Treat Context as Paramount

To determine what the leader needs to do (or not do) to be more effective and make the team more successful, context is key. The context within which the leader operates must be understood so the development initiative can be tailored. The four major elements to consider are the following:

1. **The leader's role:** Which leadership domains, dimensions, and behaviors from the Hogan Leadership Model are the most important to succeed in the role?

   For example, the behaviors required for a leader in a marketing role are very different than the ones required for a leader in a tax attorney's role.

2. **The leader's team:** What is the team's experience level? Dynamics? Morale? Motivation level?

   For example, a team of inexperienced "newbies" will have much different needs from their leader than a team of experienced professionals.

3. **The leader's manager:** What is the personality of the leader's manager? Their values? Their likes and dislikes?

For example, if a leader is high Colorful and their manager is high Colorful as well, the manager might view the leader as very entertaining, whereas a manager who is low Colorful might view the leader as a "showboat."

4. **The organization's culture:** What "is it like around here"? Which behaviors are rewarded? What are the taboos?

   For example, behaviors that are derailers in one culture might not be derailers in another. High Imaginative might be a derailer in a staid engineering culture but essential for performance in an advertising agency if managed appropriately.

Hogan coaching incorporates context throughout the initiative. The initiative begins with a context meeting between the coach, the leader's manager, and HR sponsor to obtain their perspectives on the reasons the leader is being coached and their views of the leader's context. This meeting is followed by a context meeting between the Hogan coach and the leader so the coach can understand the leader's perspective. Only after the coach conducts these meetings and understands the leader's context can the coach tailor the coaching initiative. Context is used throughout the remainder of the coaching initiative in interpreting the assessment data, determining 360 interview questions, creating the most impactful development goals, and developing the coaching session content.

Element 6
Shortfall: Neglecting the Psychology of Behavior Change
Hogan Solution: Change Is Hard; Make It Easier

Change is hard. It has been said that behavior change requires two people—one to do it and one to notice. A lack of ongoing feedback is often a problem because positive reinforcement is key to motivating change.

Many leadership development and coaching programs overlook the fact that long-term behavioral change requires leaders to have both the motivation and the ability to change. Unrealistic goals, limited resources (including time and energy), and a lack of feedback can inhibit a leader's successful development. This can be demotivating, which is especially problematic if a leader is ambivalent to development or struggles with self-awareness in the first place.

At Hogan, we believe behavior change is made easier via the following steps, and we incorporate them into our coaching protocol:

1. Increase the leader's strategic self-awareness regarding their reputation versus their identity. This is done using Hogan's assessments.

2. Connect the needed changes to achieving the reputation they want to establish.

3. Confront any ambivalence the leader has around behavior change. If the leader feels that they must give up a behavior that has made them successful thus far, they may be reluctant to do so. Assure them that they need not abandon a behavior completely but, rather, need to make subtle adjustments.

4. Find ways to make development easier using the following approaches:

   • Increase **motivation** to change the behavior.

   • Decrease the **difficulty** of changing the behavior.

   • Increase the **ability** to perform the behavior correctly.

   • Increase the **reward** for the behavior.

   • Build in cues to **prompt** the behavior.

5. Connect the needed changes to a business goal that is important to the leader and their team.

6. Find a "hook" that will motivate the leader to change. The leader's Hogan results can provide insight into this (e.g., a person with high Altruism might resonate with a behavior change will help people be more successful, or a high Ambition leader might adopt a behavior change that accelerates achieving results).

7. Clearly define the needed changes and what they look like in the leader's everyday world.

8. Select behavior changes that are not resource constrained, as time and effort are always at a premium. Identify development activities the leader can practice as part of their job, not as an add-on to their busy schedule. If a leader needs to enhance their communication skills, they should practice in their staff meetings rather than take a public speaking course.

9. Start with small pivots and baby steps, not giant steps. Many times, development goals are flawed due to the following common mistakes:

   • Goals are unrealistic.

   • Goals are too vague or too broad.

   • Results are not measurable.

   • The leader lacks the ability.

10. Look for early wins that will reinforce the value of the behavior change.

11. Encourage the leader to enlist a trusted colleague to provide honest feedback continuously.

12. Consider conducting a "pulse check" with selected stakeholders at the midway point of the coaching initiative to gauge progress.

Element 7
Shortfall: Decoupling Assessment and Development Activities
Hogan Solution: Fix the Broken Link between Assessment and Development Activities

Too often, leadership development involves an assessment or two; creating a development plan, some learning experiences, or skill building; and perhaps a coaching component. If these do not connect, the overall program is doomed to be less than maximally effective.

Instead, think about working with a personal trainer. The first step, assessment, gives the trainer the information they need to offer the leader personalized education and design a unique fitness plan for them to apply. If the trainer is effective, each new component will build on the previous one. Then the trainer will check in on the leader's progress regularly, adjusting as needed.

The Hogan coach resembles a personal trainer. The coach customizes the initiative throughout the journey and makes adjustments as needed. Leaders first acquire self-knowledge through assessment feedback, gaining an understanding of how others perceive their strengths and opportunities for improvement. With their coach, they determine which behavior changes will be most impactful for them personally, their team, and the broader organization. They then incorporate both the assessment insights and prioritized behavior changes into their development plans. Assessment, learning, development, and behavior change become a "thread" through their leadership journey.

The Hogan Coaching Protocol

In the preceding section, we discussed seven shortfalls of leadership development and how Hogan coaching addresses them. In this section, we describe the Hogan coaching protocol step by step, relating each to fixing the seven shortfalls. Each step in the protocol incorporates **almost all** fixes to ensure the coaching initiative is successful. The protocol described next, and shown in Table 35, is for a typical 6-month executive coaching initiative. The fixes associated with each step are shown in Figure 4.

Table 35: The Hogan Coaching Protocol

Coach Selection

- Chemistry Call between Coach and Leader

Phase 1: Context Gathering

Context Call between Coach, Leader's Manager, and HR Sponsor

Get-Acquainted Call between Coach and Leader

Phase 2: Assessment and Feedback

Hogan Assessments and 360 Interviews

Integrated Feedback Session

Phase 3: Development Planning

Development Planning Meeting

Development Plan Finalization Meeting

Development Plan Alignment Meeting

Phase 4: Behavior Modification and Skill-Building

Ongoing Coaching Sessions

Phase 5: Evaluation and Ensuring Continued Success

Follow-up 360 Interviews

Wrap-Up Meeting between Leader, Coach, Leader's Manager, and HR Sponsor

---

Pre-Coaching: Coach Selection

Chemistry Call

The relationship between the coach and the leader is crucial to the success of a coaching initiative. It is essential that the leader trusts the coach, feels comfortable opening up to the coach, respects what the coach recommends, and feels a sense of compatibility with the coach overall. In short, a "bond" or "chemistry" is needed between the two for coaching to be maximally successful. We provide four to six coach bios to the leader, who chooses two to three with whom they would like to have a brief "chemistry call" to check for fit. Typically, the calls are 30 minutes or less, but they enable the leader to determine

Hogan Leadership Development Solution	Chemistry Call	Context Call	Get-Acquainted Call	Hogan LFS Assessments	360 Interviews	Integrated Feedback Session	Development Planning Meeting	Development Plan Creation	Development Plan Alignment	Ongoing Coaching Sessions	Follow-up 360 Interviews	Wrap-up Meeting
Redefine Leadership		●	●	●	●	●	●	●	●	●	●	●
Measure Relevant Outcomes		●	●	●	●	●	●	●	●	●	●	●
Refocus on Steady Targets		●	●	●	●	●	●	●	●	●	●	●
Leverage Individual Differences	●		●	●	●	●	●	●	●	●	●	●
Treat Context as Paramount	●	●	●	●	●	●	●	●	●	●	●	●
Make Change Easier			●	●	●	●	●	●	●	●	●	●
Fix the Broken Link						●	●	●	●	●	●	●

Figure 4 Mapping of Leadership Development Solutions to the Hogan Coaching Protocol

which coach best meets their individual personality, context, and overall needs. Once the leader chooses a coach, the coaching initiative can begin.

Phase 1: Context Gathering

☐ *Context Call*

We involve key stakeholders, such as the leader's manager and HR sponsor, throughout the coaching process. This ensures that all parties are aligned regarding what needs to be accomplished during the coaching so there are no surprises at the end of the engagement. To obtain background and context, the coach meets with the leader's manager and HR sponsor to gain their perspective on topics such as the following:

1. Background on the organization, including culture, business goals and objectives, and challenges

2. The reason for identifying the leader for coaching

3. The leader's key strengths, areas for development, and blind spots

4. The leader's reputation

5. Behaviors most important for the leader to modify or leverage to positively impact the team

6. The leader's attitude toward coaching and feedback and their coachability

7. The leader's performance and potential within the organization

8. How they define "success" for the coaching initiative

☐ *Get-Acquainted Call*

Soon after the context call with the manager and HR sponsor, the coach and leader connect to get better acquainted. Although they meet during the chemistry call, this get-acquainted call provides an opportunity to bond further. The context call with the manager and HR sponsor provided the coach with their perspectives, and this call provides the coach with the leader's perspective on many of the same topics. Typical topics include the following:

1. Background (a brief life history), including personal and career aspects

2. Career aspirations

3. Context within which they are operating

4. View of their key strengths, areas for development, and motivators and values

5. View of their reputation

6. Major business objectives and challenges

7. Assessment of their team's ability and performance level and how they can most positively impact it

8. Understanding of why they were selected for or requested coaching

9. Definition of success of the coaching initiative

10. Concerns or questions about the coaching initiative

Phase 2: Assessment and Feedback

☐ *Hogan Assessments and 360 Interviews*

After the get-acquainted meeting, the leader takes the HPI, the HDS, and the MVPI assessments, and their respective individual reports are generated. These assessments are complemented by the coach conducting 360 interviews with key stakeholders identified by the leader and approved by the leader's manager and HR sponsor.

After the leader advises the 360 audience that they will be hearing from the coach, the coach contacts each respondent (typically 8–10) and asks them questions about the leader's strengths, areas for development, and leadership style in general.

☐ *Integrated Feedback Session*

The word to be emphasized in this step is *integrated* because by integrating the results from the Hogan assessments and the comments from the 360 interviews, a clear picture of strengths, areas for development, and blind spots is obtained. The 360 interviews reveal how the Hogan results manifest in the real world. The combination provides powerful insights into behaviors that need to be leveraged or modified and how easy or difficult it will be for the leader to change them.

Phase 3: Development Planning

☐ *Development Planning Meeting*

Although major takeaways will be identified during the integrated feedback session, it is typically premature to decide on the key development goals at this time. The leader needs to reflect on the feedback and discuss it with the coach to determine which behavior changes will be most impactful for their team and the broader business. We recommend selecting two or three development goals that are either strengths to leverage, items to watch out for and rein in, or blind spots to address. Setting more than three goals can spread the leader's efforts too thin to make noticeable progress.

☐ *Development Plan Finalization Meeting*

Typically, after the development planning meeting, the leader sends the first draft of their plan to the coach, who makes suggestions and sends it back; several iterations of this process can occur. By the final meeting, the development plan should be almost done, so the goal is to "polish" the plan to share with the leader's manager and HR sponsor. The development plan is an ideal vehicle to "Fix the Broken Link," as the goals and actions, as well as the measures of success, are connected to the team, the business, and the learning experience. It is key that the leader feels ownership for the development plan, so they need to be the author of it, with the coach providing advice and counsel.

☐ *Development Plan Alignment Meeting*

It is crucial that the leader, coach, leader's manager, and HR sponsor agree regarding the development goals selected by the leader. This four-way meeting is a chance for the leader to present their development plan, share the reasons for the selected areas as far as the team and business impact, ask for resources and support, obtain input and suggestions, and gain overall alignment on the path forward. Furthermore, the alignment meeting creates ownership of the plan and the behavior changes the leader needs because the leader presents the plan, not the coach.

Phase 4: Behavior Modification and Skill Building

☐ *Ongoing Coaching Sessions*

Once the development plan is in place, 1-hour coaching sessions occur every month for 5 months. The leader and coach determine their own rhythm, so sessions may be held twice a month for 30 minutes or an hour, depending on the leader's preferences or needs. The key is to have sessions often enough that behavior changes stay top of mind but not so often that the leader does not have time to practice new behaviors between sessions.

During these sessions, coaches apply their coaching skills to ensure progress is being made. The coaching sessions are tailored to the leader based on the development plan content and the leader's learning style. Sessions can involve the leader using the coach as a sounding board for the structured content, such as role-playing for an upcoming encounter or event.

Phase 5: Evaluation and Ensuring Continued Success

☐ *Follow-Up 360 Interviews*

In keeping with the "Measure Relevant Outcomes" solution for which Hogan recommends quantitative measures, we recommend that after the coaching sessions are completed, a brief follow-up 360 interview be conducted with the original respondents to evaluate the leader's progress.

☐ *Wrap-Up Meeting*

After the coach and leader discuss the results from the follow-up 360 interviews, they meet with the leader's manager and HR sponsor for a wrap-up session. In this meeting, the leader reviews their progress versus their development plan, including what they have learned during the coaching initiative, what is going well, and what is still left to do.

By following the Hogan coaching protocol that addresses the reasons leadership development fails, the coach can turbocharge the coaching journey so that the leader achieves significant positive impact on their effectiveness and that of their team and organization as a whole. Hogan Press's book *Coaching the Hogan Way* (Kellett & Sahm, 2024) includes a comprehensive case study for applying the Hogan coaching protocol.

Bibliography

Allport, G. W. (1961). Pattern and growth in personality. New York, NY: Holt, Rinehart and Winston.

Allport, G. W., Vernon, P. E., & Lindzey, G. (1960). *Study of values* (3rd ed.). Boston, MA: Houghton-Mifflin.

American Psychiatric Association. (1987). *Diagnostic and statistical manual of mental disorders* (3rd ed., rev.). Washington, DC: American Psychiatric Association.

American Psychiatric Association. (1994). *Diagnostic and statistical manual of mental disorders* (4th ed.). Washington, DC: American Psychiatric Association.

Americans with Disabilities Act of 1990 102(b)(7), 42 U.S.C.A. 12112.

Arthur Jr., W., Day, E. A., McNelly, T. L., & Edens, P. S. (2003). A meta-analysis of the criterion-related validity of assessment center dimensions. *Personnel Psychology, 56*(1), 125–153. https://doi.org/10.1111/j.1744-6570.2003.tb00146.x

Bentz, V. J. (1985, August). *A view from the top: A thirty-year perspective of research devoted to discovery, description, and prediction of executive behavior.* Paper presented at the 93rd Annual Convention of the American Psychological Association, Los Angeles, CA.

Boudreaux, M. J., Ferrell, B. T., Hundley, N. A., & Sherman, R. A. (2021). A personality-based measure of employability. *Journal of Personnel Psychology, 21*(1), 1–12. https://doi.org/10.1027/1866-5888/a000283

Butcher, J. N., Dahlstrom, W. G., Graham, J. R., Tellegen, A., & Kaemmer, B. (1989). *Minnesota Multiphasic Personality Inventory (MMPI-2): Manual for administration and scoring.* Minneapolis, MN: University of Minnesota Press.

Dilchert, S., Ones, D. S., Davis, R. D., & Rostow, C. D. (2007). Cognitive ability predicts objectively measured counterproductive work behaviors. *Journal of Applied Psychology, 92*(3), 616–627. https://doi.org/10.1037/0021-9010.92.3.616

Gottfredson, G. D., & Holland, J. L. (1996). *Dictionary of Holland occupational codes* (3rd ed.). Odessa, FL: Psychological Assessment Resources.

Gough, H. G. (1975). *Manual for the California Psychological Inventory* (rev. ed.). Palo Alto, CA: Consulting Psychologists Press.

Gregory, S. (1992, May). *Noncognitive measures for Army technical training placement.* Paper presented at the Seventh Annual Meeting of the Society for Industrial-Organizational Psychology, Inc. Montreal, Canada.

Hase, H. D., & Goldberg, L. R. (1967). Comparative validity of different strategies of constructing personality inventory scales. *Psychological Bulletin, 67*(4), 231–248. https://doi.org/10.1037/h0024421

Hathaway, S. R., & McKinley, J. C. (1943). *Manual for the Minnesota Multiphasic Personality Inventory.* New York, NY: Psychological Corporation.

Hazucha, J. F. (1991). *Success, jeopardy, and performance: Contrasting managerial outcomes and their predictors.* (Unpublished doctoral dissertation). University of Minnesota, Minneapolis, MN.

Heimann, A. L., Ingold, P. V., Debus, M. E., et al. (2021). Who will go the extra mile? Selecting organizational citizens with a personality-based structured job interview. *Journal of Business Psychology, 36*, 985–1007. https://doi.org/10.1007/s10869-020-09716-1

Highhouse, S. (2008). Stubborn reliance on intuition and subjectivity in employee selection. *Industrial and Organizational Psychology, 1*(3), 333–342. https://doi.org/10.1111/j.1754-9434.2008.00058.x

Hogan, R., & Blickle, G. (2013). Socioanalytic theory. In N. D. Christiansen & R. P. Tett (Eds.), *Handbook of personality at work* (pp. 53–70). New York, NY: Routledge.

Hogan, J., Hogan, R., & Kaiser, R. B. (2011). Management derailment. In S. Zedeck (Ed.), *APA handbook of industrial and organizational psychology, Vol. 3. Maintaining, expanding, and contracting the organization* (pp. 555–575). American Psychological Association. https://doi.org/10.1037/12171-015

Hogan, R., Hogan, J., & Roberts, B. W. (1996). Personality measurement and employment decisions: Questions and answers. *American Psychologist, 51*(5), 469–477. https://doi.org/10.1037/0003-066X.51.5.469

Hogan, J., & Holland, B. (2003). Using theory to evaluate personality and job-performance relations: A socio-analytic perspective. *Journal of Applied Psychology, 88*(1), 100–112. https://doi.org/10.1037/0021-9010.88.1.100

Holland, J. L. (1966). *The psychology of vocational choice: A theory of personality types and model environments.* Waltham, MA: Ginn.

Holland, J. L. (1985). *Making vocational choices: A theory of vocational personalities and work environments* (2nd ed.). Englewood Cliffs, NJ: Prentice-Hall.

Holland, J. L. (1987). *1987 manual supplement for the Self-Directed Search.* Odessa, FL: Psychological Assessment Resources.

Horney, K. (1950). *Neurosis and human growth.* New York, NY: Norton.

Hough, L. M. (2001). I/Owes its advances to personality. In B. W. Roberts & R. Hogan (Eds.), *Personality psychology in the workplace* (pp. 19–44). American Psychological Association. https://doi.org/10.1037/10434-001

John, O. P. (2021). History, measurement, and conceptual elaboration of the Big Five trait taxonomy: The paradigm matures. In O. P. John & R. W. Robins (Eds.), *Handbook of personality: Theory and research* (4th ed., pp. 35–82). New York, NY: The Guilford Press.

Jones, A. B., Sherman, R. A., & Hogan, R. T. (2017). Where is ambition in factor models of personality? *Personality and Individual Differences, 106*, 26–31. https://doi.org/10.1016/j.paid.2016.09.057

Jones, W. H. (1988). *User's manual for PROFILE.* Unpublished report.

Kellett, T., & Sahm, J. (2024). *Coaching the Hogan Way.* Tulsa, OK: Hogan Press.

LePine, J. A., & Van Dyne, L. (2001). Voice and cooperative behavior as contrasting forms of contextual performance: evidence of differential relationships with big five personality characteristics and cognitive ability. *Journal of Applied Psychology, 86*(2), 326–336. https://doi.org/10.1037/0021-9010.86.2.326

Lombardo, M. M., Ruderman, M. N., & McCauley, C. D. (1988). Explanations of success and derailment in upper-level management positions. *Journal of Business and Psychology, 2*(3), 199–216. https://doi.org/10.1007/BF01014038

Mabon, H. (1998). Utility Aspects of Personality and Performance. *Human Performance, 11*(2-3), 289–304. https://doi.org/10.1080/08959285.1998.9668035

McCall, M. W., Jr., & Lombardo, M. M. (1983). *Off the track: Why and how successful executives get derailed* (Tech. Rep. No. 21). Greensboro, NC: Center for Creative Leadership.

McDaniel, M. A., Whetzel, D. L., Schmidt, F. L., & Maurer, S. D. (1994). The validity of employment interviews: A comprehensive review and meta-analysis. *Journal of Applied Psychology, 79*(4), 599–616. https://doi.org/10.1037/0021-9010.79.4.599

Murray, H. A. (1938). *Explorations in personality: A clinical and experimental study of fifty men of college age.* New York, NY: The Oxford University Press.

Novacek, J., and Lazarus, R. S. (1990). The structure of personal commitments. *Journal of Personality, 58*, 693–715. https://doi.org/10.1111/j.1467-6494.1990.tb00250.x

O'Boyle, E. H., Forsyth, D. R., Banks, G. C., Story, P. A., & White, C. D. (2015). A meta-analytic test of redundancy and relative importance of the dark triad and five-factor model of personality. *Journal of Personality, 83*(6), 644–664. https://doi.org/10.1111/jopy.12126

Pervin, L. A. (Ed.). (1989). *Goal concepts in personality and social psychology.* Hillsdale, NJ: Lawrence Erlbaum Associates, Inc.

Richards, J. M., Jr. (1966). Life goals of American college freshmen. *Journal of Counseling Psychology*, *13*(1), 12–20. https://doi.org/10.1037/h0023049

Roberts, B. W., Kuncel, N. R., Shiner, R., Caspi, A., & Goldberg, L. R. (2007). The Power of Personality: The Comparative Validity of Personality Traits, Socioeconomic Status, and Cognitive Ability for Predicting Important Life Outcomes. *Perspectives on Psychological Science*, *2*(4), 313–345. https://doi.org/10.1111/j.1745-6916.2007.00047.x

Spranger, E. (1928). *Types of men: The psychology and ethics of personality*. Halle: Max Niemeyer Verlag.

Thurstone, L. L. (1934). The vectors of mind. *Psychological Review*, *41*(1), 1–32. https://doi.org/10.1037/h0075959

Tupes, E. C., & Christal, R. E. (1961). Recurrent personality factors based on trait ratings (Tech. Rep. No. ASD-TR-61-97). Lackland Air Force Base, TX: Aeronautical Systems Division, Personnel Laboratory.

U.S. Department of Labor. (1991). *Dictionary of occupational titles* (4th ed., rev.). U.S. Government Printing Office.

Wicker, F. W., Lambert, F. B., Richardson, F. C., & Kahler, J. (1984). Categorical goal hierarchies and classification of human motives. *Journal of Personality*, *52*(3), 285–305. https://doi.org/10.1111/j.1467-6494.1984.tb00883.x

Wiggins, J. S. (1979). A psychological taxonomy of trait-descriptive terms: The interpersonal domain. *Journal of Personality and Social Psychology*, *37*(3), 395–412. https://doi.org/10.1037/0022-3514.37.3.395

Winterberg, C. A., Tapia, M. A., Nei, K. S., & Brummel, B. J. (2019). A clarification of ADA jurisprudence for personality-based selection. *Industrial and Organizational Psychology*, *12*(2), 172–176. https://doi:10.1017/iop.2019.34

Index

A

Accomplishment, 19, 56, 57, 60, 80, 81, 82, 85

Adjustment, 9, 14, 15, 16, 92, 102, 106, 109, 111, 116, 117, 120, 121, 128, 149, 150

Aesthetics, 73, 75, 96, 97, 109, 111, 113, 114, 119

Affiliation, 73, 74, 88, 89, 111, 112, 113, 120, 122

Agreeableness, 8, 54

Altruistic, 73, 74, 86, 87, 111, 119, 122, 123

Ambition, 8, 9, 17–18, 19, 73, 102-103, 106, 107, 109, 111, 112–113, 114, 116, 117, 120-123, 128, 149

Arrogance, 68, 118, 121

Assessment Results, 130

Avoidant, 38, 39, 51, 59, 92

Avoids Trouble, 28

B

Beliefs, 3, 38, 40, 42, 47, 75, 76, 90

Bold, 17, 20, 38, 56–57, 68, 69, 111, 112, 116, 118, 121, 122–123, 128

Bright Side, 2, 8, 132

C

California Psychological Inventory (CPI), 8

Calmness, 16

Career-derailing Tendencies, 47

Caring, 25, 52

Cautious, 26, 28, 38, 50–51, 68, 93, 109, 113, 114, 118, 120–121, 133

Center for Creative Leadership, 41

Colorful, 21, 38, 60–61, 68, 69, 109, 111, 118, 148

Commerce, 73, 75, 94–95, 111, 112-113, 119

Competitive, 9, 17, 19, 73, 82, 83, 94, 103, 107, 112, 116, 117, 122

Conforming, 8, 26, 58, 66, 67, 75

Conscientiousness, 4, 8, 68, 107

Creative Thinking, 63

Culture, 4, 11, 31, 43, 72, 76, 80, 81, 83, 84, 85, 87, 89, 90, 91, 93, 95, 97, 99, 119, 128, 132, 133, 148, 152

Curiosity, 31, 105

Cynical, 38, 48–49, 54

D

Dark Side, 2, 132

Data integration, 127, 137, 138

Diligent, 39, 64–65, 68, 69, 109, 111, 112–113, 114, 118, 119, 121

Distractable, 61

DSM-IV, 37, 39

DSM-IV Axis 38-39

Dutiful, 26, 39, 66–67, 68, 69, 111, 112, 113, 118, 119

E

Easily Disappointed, 47

Easy to Live With, 25

Eccentric, 38, 62, 63, 68, 87

Education, 32-33, 34

Empathy, 16, 136

Employee Development, 33

Employee Selection, 8, 76

Entertaining, 22, 60, 85, 148

Entitled, 56, 57, 106

Even-Tempered, 14, 16, 46

Excitable, 38, 46–47, 68, 111, 118, 120

Exhibitionistic, 22

Experience Seeking, 22

Extraversion, 8, 9

F

Fantasized Talent, 57

Fearful, 39, 51

Five Factor Model (FFM), 8–9

Freud, Sigmund, 36-37

G

Generates Ideas, 29, 31, 106
Good Attachment, 16
Good Memory, 34
Grudges, 48, 49

H

Hedonism, 73, 74, 84–85, 109, 111, 112
Hedonistic, 73, 74
High Scorers, 48, 50, 54, 89, 90, 92, 94, 96, 98
Hogan Assessments, 2, 3, 126, 130, 136, 137, 151, 153–154
Hogan Coaching Network (HCN), 126
Hogan Development Survey (HDS), 2, 5, 36, 38–39, 118–119, 132
Hogan Personality Inventory (HPI), 2, 5, 8, 132
Homogenous Item Composites (HICs), 9–10, 11, 15, 18, 21, 24, 27, 30, 33, 42
Human Nature, 2

I

Identity, 18, 19, 72, 90, 130, 148
Imaginative, 9, 29, 30, 38, 62-63, 68–69, 75, 92, 111, 112, 113
Impulse Control, 28
Impulsive, 20, 28, 56, 58–59, 68, 90, 96, 104, 105, 106, 113, 122
Indecisive, 18, 50, 54, 66, 67
Ingratiating, 67, 113
Inquisitive, 29-30, 31, 103, 104, 105, 106, 107, 108, 109, 111, 113, 117
Intellectual Games, 31
Interpersonal Sensitivity, 23–24, 25, 55, 104, 108, 111, 113, 114, 116, 117, 122, 127
Introverted, 53, 112
Irritated, 16, 38, 55

J

Job Performance, 3-5, 9, 32, 33, 40, 43, 116, 118

K

Kaizen Psychometrics, 10, 40

L

Languages, 8, 10, 11, 43, 77, 97
Leadership, 17, 18, 19, 56, 74, 76, 81, 83, 85, 87, 89, 91, 93, 95, 97, 99, 127, 130–131, 142-146, 149, 155

Learning Approach, 32–33, 34, 109, 111, 112
Leisurely, 38, 54–55, 68, 69, 111, 112, 113, 114, 118, 119
Likes Crowds, 22
Likes Parties, 22
Likes People, 25
Low Scorers, 54, 92, 94, 96, 98

M

Managers, 4, 14, 94-99, 116
Manipulative, 38, 58, 59
Mastery, 28
Math Ability, 34
Minnesota Multiphasic Personality Inventory (MMPI), 36
Mischievous, 38, 58–59, 68, 69, 109, 111, 112, 113, 118, 119, 123, 133
Mistrusting, 49
Moralistic, 28
Motivation, 72, 74, 77, 121, 147, 148, 149
Motives, Values, Preferences Inventory (MVPI), 2, 5, 72, 132
Moving Against, 37, 42, 68, 118
Moving Away, 37, 42, 68, 118
Moving Toward, 37, 42, 68, 118

N

Neuroticism, 8
No Complaints, 16
No Direction, 47
No Guilt, 16
No Hostility, 25, 127
No Social Anxiety, 19
Not Anxious, 16, 103
Not Autonomous, 28
Not Spontaneous, 28

O

Openness to Experience, 8, 9
Organized, 65
Overconfidence, 57

P

Passive Aggressive, 38, 55
Perfectionistic, 64, 65
Personality Assessment, 2, 3, 4, 8, 9, 36, 37
Personality Characteristics, 2, 116, 121, 122, 134

Personality Profiles, 11, 109
Personality Psychology, 2, 8
Personnel Decisions International, 41
Power, 56, 72-74, 82-83, 102, 111
PROFILE, 40
Prudence, 20-28, 103–109, 111, 112–113, 116, 117, 120–122
Public Confidence, 61

R
Reading, 34
Recognition, 57, 72, 73, 80–81, 111
Reserved, 21, 38, 39, 52–53, 68, 80, 88, 104, 107, 109, 111, 113, 118, 123
Risky, 59

S
Science, 73, 75, 98–99, 111, 114, 119, 126, 127, 134
Science Ability, 31
Security, 41, 68, 73, 74–75, 92–93, 109, 111, 112, 122, 123
Self-Confident, 16, 19, 38, 106, 112, 121
Self-Display, 60, 61
Sensitive, 15, 23–24, 25, 39, 41, 46, 75, 86, 113, 118
Skeptical, 33, 38, 39, 48–49, 68, 111
Social, 110

Sociability, 9, 111, 112, 113, 114, 117, 120, 122, 128
Socioanalytic Theory, 2, 9
Special Sensitivity, 63
Standards, 65
Syndromes, 68, 112, 114

T
Talent Management, 2, 3, 4, 40
Teams, 36, 53, 66, 76, 82, 83, 84, 88-89, 90, 92, 94, 97, 98, 99, 130
Thrill Seeking, 31
Tough, 52-53, 67, 86, 104
Tradition, 29, 73, 74, 109, 111, 112, 113, 119
Trust, 14, 16, 23, 24, 27, 98, 135
Trusting, 14, 16, 48–49

U
Unappreciated, 55
Unassertive, 18, 50, 51, 57, 111
Unsocial, 53

V
Validation Research, 11, 44, 78
Validity, 3, 9, 10, 40, 41, 44, 76
Virtuous, 28
Volatile, 46, 47

www.ingramcontent.com/pod-product-compliance
Lightning Source LLC
Chambersburg PA
CBHW081815200326
41597CB00023B/4263